THE 100+ SERIES™

Reproducible Activities

Nonfiction
Reading Comprehension

Grades 3-4

By
Gail Blasser Riley

Cover Design by
Matthew Van Zomeren

Inside Illustrations by
Jill Wood

Published by Instructional Fair • TS Denison
an imprint of

McGraw-Hill
Children's Publishing

About the Author

Gail Blasser Riley, an award-wining author, has written more than 200 books, articles, poems, and greeting verses for adults and children of all ages. Gail has taught classes from preschool through the graduate level. She also frequently writes and edits educational material and is the author of McGraw-Hill Children's Publishing's *Cause and Effect* for grades 3–4. Gail visits educators and students across the country as an educational consultant. She has also served as Regional Advisor for the Society of Children's Book Writers and Illustrators. She is coauthor of their "Directory Guide to Educational Markets."

Credits

Author: Gail Blasser Riley
Inside Illustrations: Jill Wood
Cover Design: Matthew Van Zomeren
Project Director/Editor: Mary Rose Hassinger
Editors: Karen Thompson, Sara Bierling
Graphic Layout: Ron Kauffman

McGraw-Hill
Children's Publishing

A Division of The **McGraw·Hill** Companies

Published by Instructional Fair • TS Denison
An imprint of McGraw-Hill Children's Publishing
Copyright © 2002 McGraw-Hill Children's Publishing

Send all inquiries to:
McGraw-Hill Children's Publishing
3195 Wilson Drive NW
Grand Rapids, Michigan 49544

All Rights Reserved • Printed in the United States of America

Nonfiction Reading Comprehension—grades 3–4
ISBN: 0-7424-0219-3

2 3 4 5 6 7 8 9 PHXBK 07 06 05 04 03

Table of Contents

Name _____

Ants, Ants Everywhere!

Directions: Read the information about fire ants and leaf cutter ants. Use what you learn to complete the Venn diagram on page 5.

Fire Ants Attack

Where does the fire ant get its name? Its bite hurts like blazing fire. Some people compare fire ants to weeds. Fire ant colonies spread like wildfire, and ants can live in all sorts of conditions. Like weeds, once fire ants have taken root, it is very hard to remove them.

Fire ants make their home in the United States and other places. They also build their mounds on the Galapagos Islands and in parts of the South Pacific. Scientists now worry that fire ants are being found in West Africa and are attacking animals there.

Leaf Cutter Ants

Unlike fire ants, leaf cutter ants are often welcome guests. They help the environment by fertilizing the soil. They chomp small half-circles from plants. Then they march to their underground colonies with this plant treasure. Underground, they chew up the plants and add them to their own garden. The plants mix with other items in the leaf-cutter underground garden. This mixture helps the soil in the rain forest.

Directions: Read the information about fire ants and leaf cutter ants on page 4. Fill in the Venn diagram telling how fire ants and leaf cutter ants are alike and how they are different according to page 4.

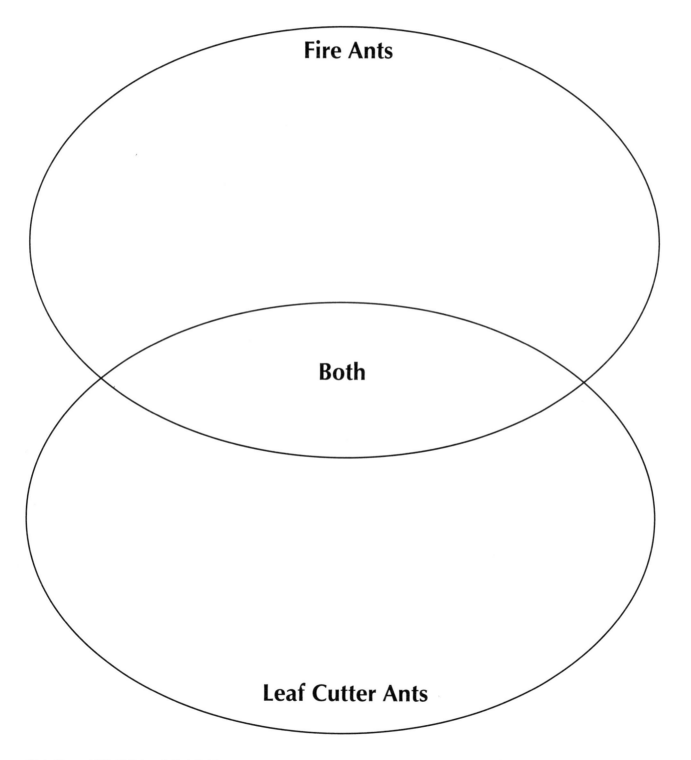

Fire Ants

Both

Leaf Cutter Ants

Name _____

Vote for Me

Directions: Juan and Samantha are both running for class officer. Here are their campaign posters. How are their posters and promises alike? How are they different? Fill in the Venn diagram below.

Vote for Juan!

I WILL:

◆ set up after school homework help

◆ work for better lunchroom food

◆ organize a car wash to make money for a class trip

◆ have class meetings each week

◆ set up field trips to the museum and zoo

◆ more P.E. equipment

I am honest and fair. I want to work for you. Please vote for me. You'll be glad you did.

My name is **Samantha** *and I'm here to say,*

"Vote for me on election day!"

I want to help you,
And you know why —
Because I'm here to work and try.

The lunchroom food will
be better, you'll see
If you will please just vote for me.

We'll all get together after
school each week.
I'm the new class president
you seek.

Vote for Samantha

Juan　　　　　**Samantha**

Both

Name _____

Volcanoes on Earth and Venus

Earth and Venus are planets that have volcanoes. Venus has more volcanoes than any other planet. Scientists have mapped more than 1,600 on Venus. Some scientists believe that there may be more than one million volcanoes on the planet.

Why do Venus and Earth both have volcanoes? These planets are alike in many ways. Some call Earth and Venus sister planets. Both have clouds and a thick atmosphere. The two are almost the same size and have almost the same mass. Venus's orbit around the Sun is much like Earth's.

Though Earth and Venus are alike in many ways, there are also many differences. Water does not exist on the surface of Venus. Venus's clouds are very high and are not made of the same material as Earth's. The temperature on Venus's surface is about 470º Centigrade, or 878º Fahrenheit, but Earth's temperatures are much cooler. Venus's clouds hold in the planet's heat. Its temperatures could melt lead.

On Earth, volcanoes erupt in a number of different ways. On Venus, however, almost all volcanoes erupt with flat lava flows. Scientists have not found information to show that many of Venus's volcanoes erupt and spew great amounts of ash into the sky.

Directions: Using the information above, fill in the Venn diagram to show how Earth and Venus are alike and different. Include information about volcanoes.

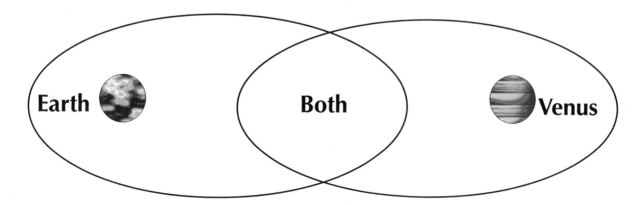

Name _____

Kelp Forests and Our Ecology

Directions: Read about kelp and rain forests. Use what you learn to answer the questions on page 9.

Rain forests are important to ecology. Kelp forests are, too. Rain forests keep many animals safe. So do kelp forests. While rain forests are on the land, kelp forests are in the ocean.

Like rain forests, kelp forests are home for many types of animals. But the kinds of animals are very different. Crab, eel, lobster, octopuses, sea horses, and sea urchin are just a few of the sea creatures that live in sea kelp.

In California alone, kelp forests are home to more than 770 animal species. A sandy ocean bottom can make a home for some creatures, but a kelp forest can make a home for thousands more. Why? The animals can live on the many kinds of kelp surfaces—rocky and leafy ones, for example.

You know about foods that come from the rain forests, like bananas. And you know about seafood that comes from sea kelp forests. You might be surprised to learn that the kelp itself is used in food such as gelatin and ice cream. Sea kelp is even used to make some varieties of toothpaste thicker.

Like a rain forest, a kelp forest has layers. You will find three main layers in a kelp forest. They are the canopy, middle, and floor layers. The canopy is at the top, and the floor is at the bottom.

You will find different sea creatures and plants at different kelp forest levels. Herring and mackerel like to swim through the canopy as do blue-rayed limpets. Sea slugs and snails feast on sea mats they find in the canopy.

Sea urchins look for food in the middle layer. Red seaweeds are often found in this layer of the kelp forest as well, though they might be found at other levels.

Sea anemones, crabs, and lobsters live on the floor level. Older blue-rayed limpets feast here, too.

Name _____

Directions: Complete this page using information from page 8.

---

1. Which creatures would you usually find in the darker part of the kelp forest, lobster or young blue-rayed limpets? How do you know?

   _____

   _____

2. How is the canopy level of the kelp forest like the canopy level of the rain forest?

   _____

   _____

   _____

3. Complete the Venn diagram to show how the rain forest and kelp forest are alike and different.

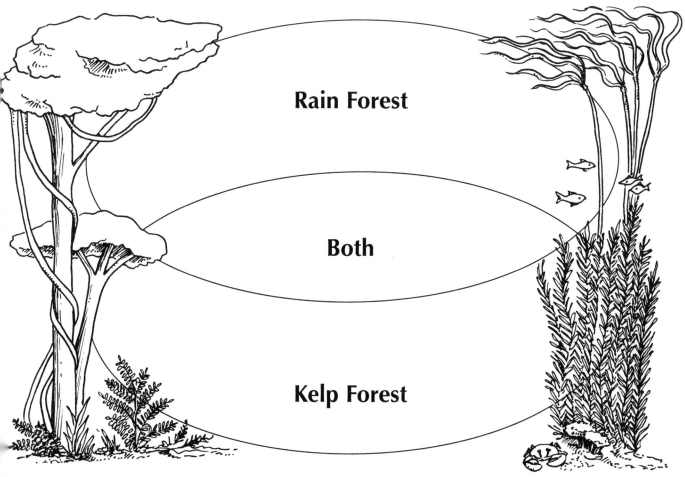

Rain Forest

Both

Kelp Forest

Name _____

Across the Great State of Texas

Texas is a huge state. The well-known cities of Dallas and Houston are both in Texas. These two cities are alike and different. Interstate 45 runs through both of these cities, and both have traffic loops so cars can drive around the entire city.

The weather in Dallas and Houston are similar during most of the year. Both cities are very hot during the summer; however, the temperature in Dallas often gets colder in the winter than in Houston. Unlike Houston, it is common for snow to fall in Dallas at least once each year. In Houston, snow almost never falls.

While Dallas and Houston both have a good deal of rain, Houston is much more likely to flood than Dallas. Houston is located at a lower level, and it is fairly close to the ocean.

Galveston has the closest beach to both Dallas and Houston. People can drive to Galveston from Houston in about an hour. But people would have to drive for many hours from Dallas to Galveston.

Both Dallas and Houston have big sports arenas. However, the Rockets play basketball for Houston and the Mavericks play basketball for Dallas.

Many people travel between the cities of Houston and Dallas to enjoy the attractions both cities have to offer.

Directions: Read the information about Dallas and Houston. Fill in the Venn diagram to tell how these cities are alike and different.

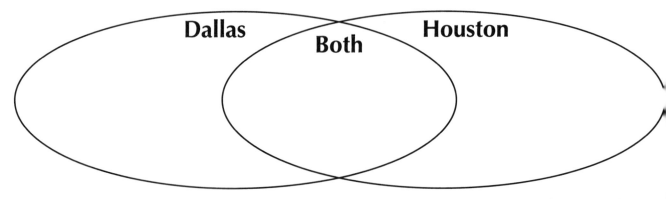

Dallas   Both   Houston

Name _____

Directions: Use what you know about comparing and contrasting to complete the activities below.

1. Complete a Venn diagram of your own. Choose which of these you would like to compare:

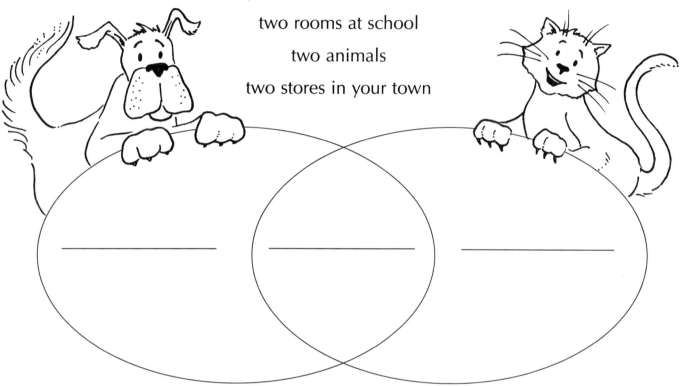

two rooms at school

two animals

two stores in your town

2. Use the information in your Venn diagram to write one paragraph. Do not forget a title and topic sentence.

_____

_____

_____

_____

_____

Name _____

Disaster!

The Hindenburg, an airship that flew in 1937, was 804 feet (245 m) long, almost as long as the Titanic! The Hindenburg did not sail the seas. It flew in the sky. It was so big that it makes airplanes of today look like small birds in the sky.

The passengers onboard the Hindenburg had beds and a reading and writing room. There were even large viewing windows to allow passengers a look at the land below as they traveled between Europe and the Unites States.

Sadly, the Hindenburg burst into flames while preparing to land on May 6, 1937, killing and injuring many people. Large airships were not built or used again. Still, the Hindenburg has become part of world history.

Directions: Use the information in the passage above and the information you already know to write a paragraph that compares and contrasts an airplane, the Hindenburg, and the Titanic. Use another sheet of paper.

Include the following points in your paragraph. After you have written your paragraph, check to be certain that you have included everything. Place a check mark by each item.

_____ at least one way in which the Hindenburg and the Titanic are alike

_____ at least one way in which the Hindenburg and an airplane are alike

_____ at least one difference between the Hindenburg and an airplane

_____ at least one difference between the Hindenburg and the Titanic

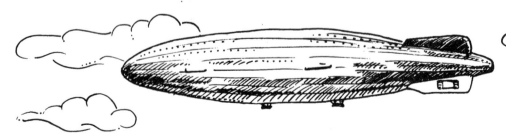

Name _____

The Underground Railroad

Directions: Read about the Underground Railroad. Use what you learn to complete the Venn diagram on page 14.

The Underground Railroad wasn't a railroad at all. It was a group of people who helped slaves escape to freedom. Those in charge of the escape effort were often called "conductors," just like the conductors of a train. The people escaping were known as "passengers," just like train passengers. And the places where the escaping slaves stopped for help were often called "stations," just like the places trains stop.

Like a train ride, the Underground Railroad moved people along, but the way in which they moved was very different from a train ride. Those who escaped often followed routes that had been laid out by others before them. However, unlike a train ride, some routes went underground through dirt tunnels without any sort of tracks.

Similar to a train ride, those traveling the Underground Railroad often traveled great distances, but they had no train seats and no gentle rocking of the train car on the tracks. Instead, they had difficult trails to follow. They rarely traveled during the day, finding that it was safer to travel at night.

Escaping slaves had to be certain that they could find their way. They needed food and water to make the journey. Conductors often helped with this. One of the most famous Underground Railroad conductors was Harriet Tubman. She had escaped slavery herself. Another famous conductor was Levi Coffin.

Experts disagree about how well the underground railroad was organized. Still, it is believed that the system helped thousands of slaves reach freedom between 1830 and 1860.

Directions: Use the information about the Underground Railroad found on page 13. Fill in the Venn diagram to tell how the Underground Railroad and railroad trains are alike and different.

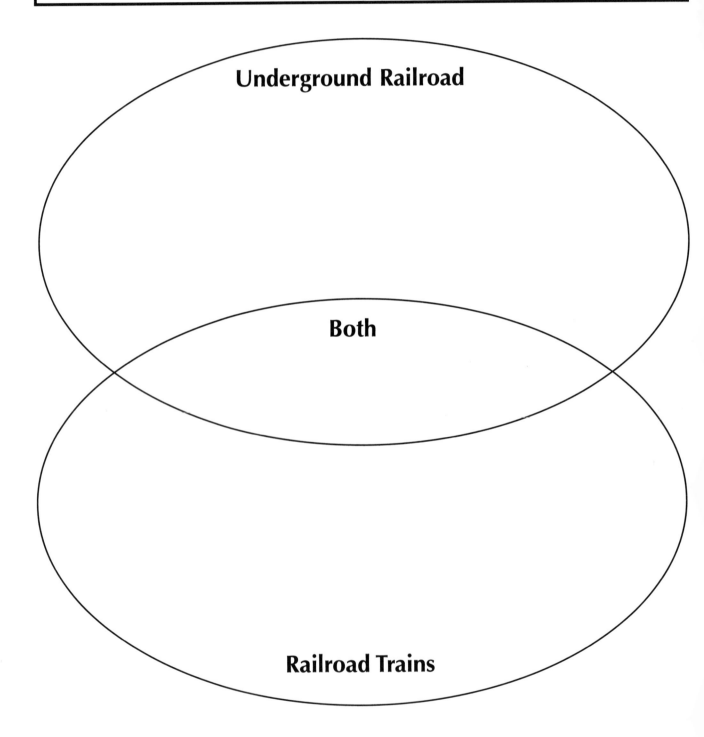

Name _____

 **Sending It Your Way**

Directions: Read the information about ways to communicate. Use this as you fill in the Venn diagram on page 16.

E-mail and letters sent with postage stamps are both alike and different. Both send information to someone. Both are forms of communication. E-mail and letters can go across the country or across the world. Both can hold large amounts of information.

The e-mail message, however, can zip across the country or the world in no time. It is sent electronically, not by people who carry it to your door. The letter can take days or weeks to get where it is going, and you must pay postage for the letter. You do not have to pay for each e-mail you send although you do pay to access the Internet.

A letter sent with a postage stamp can have a personal signature. You can enclose photographs. If you have the right equipment, you attach photographs with an e-mail.

People have been able to send mail with postage stamps for many decades. E-mail is much newer. Sometimes, other people can read the information in your e-mail. The information can be stored in a computer system for a very long time, even as long as the computer system exists. But when you send a letter with a postage stamp, it is not stored anywhere and is usually only seen by the person to whom it is addressed.

If you have problems with your computer or the Internet, you cannot send an e-mail. You must wait until your service is working again. If you want to send a letter with a postage stamp, you can find any mailbox to mail it. You do not have to rely on your computer.

Both e-mail and letters sent with postage stamps are good ways to communicate. It is important to choose which works better for you and for each message you send.

15

Directions: Use the information on page 15 to fill in the Venn diagram telling how e-mails and mail are alike and different.

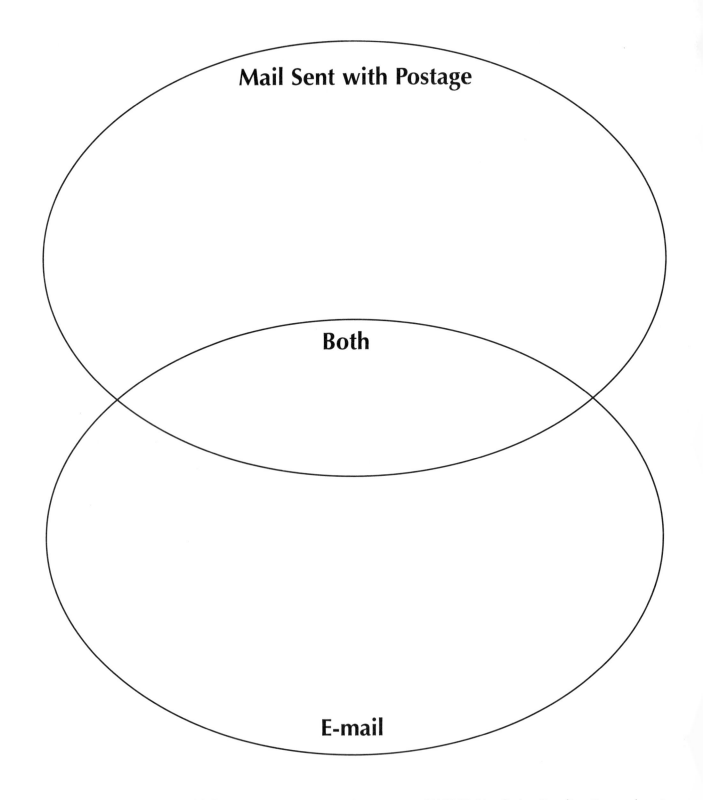

Mail Sent with Postage

Both

E-mail

Name _____

A Honey of a Job

Can you imagine having two stomachs, one that is just for honey? That is exactly what honey bees have. They need a place to store nectar. The honey bee's tongue is like a straw. The bee uses its tongue to suck nectar. Then the nectar goes to the bee's stomach.

Can you imagine having a stomach that weighs almost as much as you do? When the honey bee's stomach is filled with honey, that is exactly what happens.

When a bee makes honey, it is making something from nature even better. The bee gathers nectar from a plant. Then it turns the nectar into honey.

A worker bee earns its name. It visits between fifty and one hundred flowers in just one journey to collect nectar. One bee spends a lifetime creating one-twelfth of a teaspoon of honey.

Suppose that all the workers in a hive create one pound of honey. The workers would need to travel an incredible 55,000 miles (85,500 km) and need to visit two million flowers to collect the necessary nectar.

Did you know that the state of Utah has the nickname *The Beehive State*? But Utah does not produce the most honey in the United States. The states that produce the most honey are South Dakota, Florida, and California.

Directions: Use the information above to complete the activities about honeybees here and on page 18. Use complete sentences when answering.

1. How many stomachs does a honeybee have?

_____

_____

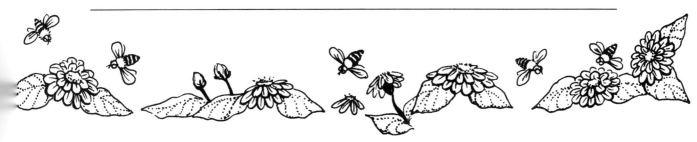

Name _____

Directions: Use the information on page 17 to complete these activities about honeybees. Use complete sentences when answering the questions.

2. How many flowers would two honeybees visit in just one journey?

   _____

   _____

3. It would take the entire lifetime of how many bees to create a full teaspoon of honey?

   _____

   _____

4. On the map above, write *The Beehive State* on the state that holds this title.

5. Draw a bee on the three states that produce the most honey in the United States.

Name _____

Native Americans of the Southwest

Directions: Read the information about Native Americans. Use what you learn to complete the following activities here and on page 20.

Apache, Navajo, Zuni, Pueblo, and Hopi are the main Southwest Native American tribes. Southwest Native Americans are known to have lived their earliest days in Colorado, Arizona, New Mexico, and Mexico.

Most early Southwest Native Americans lived in farming villages. They not only produced farm crops, but beautiful baskets, clothing, and pottery. The pottery had many uses, including food preparation and storage.

But one of the most interesting uses of the pottery was the story the individual pieces told. Native Americans carved and painted designs on many pieces. These designs were not only beautiful but helped tell family and tribal stories.

Native Americans are also well-known for producing beautiful pieces of turquoise jewelry. This stone is referred to as the stone of happiness, health, and good fortune.

---

1. The passage tells you about the places Southwest Native Americans lived. Draw a basket or piece of pottery in each of these places on the map. If you need help, use an atlas.

Directions: Use what you have learned on page 19 to complete the following activities.

2. You have read that Native Americans told stories on pieces of pottery. Write a story describing a day a Native American might have spent farming or making jewelry, baskets, pottery, or clothing. Draw the details of the story on the pottery below.

Name _____

Dancing the Day Away

Directions: Read the information. Then look at pictures A and B. Each one shows a type of bee "dance." Use what you have learned to answer the questions on page 22.

If you had just eaten at a good restaurant, you might tell your friends about it. You might tell your friends what the food tasted like and where they could find the restaurant. Bees cannot communicate the way you do, of course.

Instead, a bee brings back a sample of nectar. The other bees can taste the nectar. But how do the other bees find out where the nectar is? Many experts believe that the returning bee does dances and buzzes to tell this information. The dances tell how far the flower is from the hive and in what direction other bees need to travel to find the flower. The dances even tell how good the nectar is, and how much nectar bees will find there.

The "round" dance tells bees that nectar is near the hive. The bee dances around in a circle.

The "waggle" dance tells bees that nectar is farther away. The dancing bee dances in two loops and then flies down the middle. Other bees can tell about distance based on how fast the dancing bee loops and how long it buzzes.

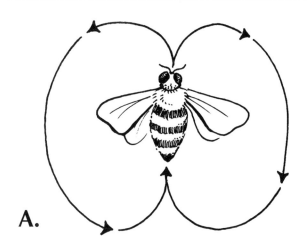

A.

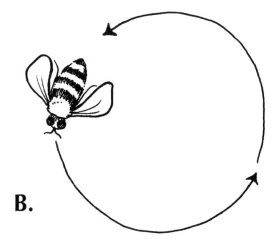

B.

Directions: Use the information on page 21 to complete these activities.

1. Which picture shows the dance that tells food is nearby the bee?

    _____

2. What is this dance called?

    _____

3. Which picture shows the dance that tells food is farther away?

    _____

4. What is this dance called?

    _____

5. In the space below, draw a returning bee doing a dance that shows
    the bees in the hive that the food supply is completely gone.

Name _____

Landforms

Directions: Read the information about landforms. Use what you have learned to complete the activity on page 24.

The world is made up of all sorts of landforms. Mountains rise up high out of the land around them. They often have steep peaks. Plains and plateaus are the opposite. They are flat. Plains are low-level flat surfaces. Plateaus are land areas that are high like mountains, but have flat tops.

An island is a body of land surrounded by water. A peninsula is similar. It is a body of land surrounded by water on only three sides.

A volcano is a cone-shaped mountain. It is formed from ash or rock that bursts up from inside the earth. There is often an opening at the top of a volcano.

A strait and an isthmus are similar, too. A strait is a narrow waterway. It connects two larger bodies of water. An isthmus is a narrow strip of land that connects two larger areas of land.

A valley is the area of land between mountains or hills. Low land makes up a valley. A swamp is also an area of low land, but it differs from a valley. Swamp land is very wet. Trees and grass grow on swamp land.

Name _____

Directions: Use the information on page 23 to help complete this activity.
Label each landform shown using the landforms mentioned in the reading.

Directions: Use the information from page 26 to complete these activities.

1. Place these events in the correct order. Number each event 1, 2, 3, or 4.

_____ Volcanic ash spews great distances.

_____ Magma forms underground pockets.

_____ Lava makes a cone-shaped mountain.

_____ Magma shoves its way through cracks in solid rock.

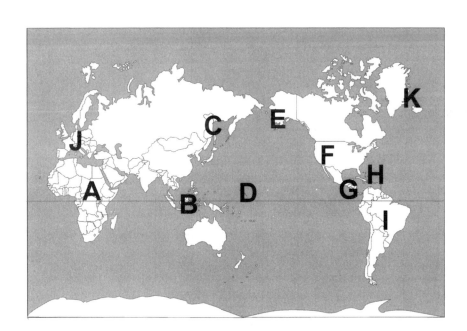

2. On this map some volcanoes are located in the ocean.

   True   False

3. On the map there are no active volcanoes shown in the United States.

   True   False

4. The letter A lets you know that there are active volcanoes in South America.

   True   False

5. The letter K tells you there are active volcanoes in Asia.

   True   False

Warning! Warning!

Hurricanes are serious storms that occur over the ocean. The tropical ocean water is warm. A low-pressure area forms above the waves, just as these areas often form during the summer and early fall. The warm, moist air zips up above the waves. Cooler air moves in. This causes the air to spin. Air pressure in the center drops. More warm, moist air is sucked up into the system. It creates wind, rain, and clouds. Inside the wall, the system's 'eye' is calm. But around the 'eye', the rain, wind, and clouds swirl in the fierce hurricane.

Hurricanes begin as tropical waves. When a storm becomes stronger, it is called a tropical depression. As its winds grow even stronger, it becomes a tropical storm, and then it can become a full-blown hurricane.

The U.S. Air Force often sends special planes into these storms to check their strength. Satellites watch them from above. The satellite images show towers of clouds building higher and higher. Hurricane warnings go out as soon as possible up and down the coastline. People get prepared for the monster storm to strike.

Directions: Use the facts above to put this list of events is order. Number the events 1, 2, 3, 4, or 5.

_____ Cooler air moves in.

_____ Hurricane warnings are issued.

_____ Summer begins.

_____ The air begins to spin.

_____ A low-pressure area forms above the waves.

Name _____

Radio: How Did It Begin?

Directions: Read about radios and use the facts to complete the activity on page 32.

Inventor Guglielmo Marconi came to the United States in 1899. Telegraph communication by wire was already in place, but Marconi wanted to show off his wireless communication—radio.

Marconi's invention could send Morse code without using any wires. He thought this would help with business communication. When introducing his work, he also planned to show how his invention could do things such as broadcasting a sporting event.

Other people had more and different ideas. These ideas led to programs being broadcast on the radio that included spoken words and music. Operas, comedy hours, and important speeches were now being heard in many homes throughout the country. Two famous radio broadcasts were: the "War of the Worlds" presentation on October 31, 1938, a fictional story that told about invading aliens, and President Roosevelt's radio announcement of the Japanese attack on Pearl Harbor, on December 8, 1941.

In 1922, there were thirty radio stations that sent broadcasts. By 1923, the number had grown to an amazing five hundred fifty-six! There was a problem with so many stations broadcasting however. There was no regular way to do things. Radio station owners organized their stations the way they saw fit.

Even though stations organized into networks, broadcasting still was not organized. The United States government passed laws to regulate radio. This let station owners know which airwaves they could use. The laws also addressed what was okay to say on the radio and what was not appropriate.

Even though television and the Internet are with us today, most homes and cars have radios. It looks as though this kind of communication is here to stay, thanks to Mr. Marconi and his invention.

Name _____

Directions: Use the information found on page 31 to help put these events in the order they happened in radio history.

Thirty radio stations were broadcasting.

Marconi came to the United States.

Laws for radio broadcasting were passed.

President Roosevelt announces the attack on Pearl Harbor.

Five hundred fifty-six radio stations were broadcasting.

The radio broadcast of the "War of the Worlds" reading.

Name _____

What Kind of Metamorphosis?

Directions: Use what you know about metamorphosis to complete the activity below.

You have read about metamorphosis. You have learned that some insects go through incomplete or gradual metamorphosis and that others go through complete metamorphosis. Here is a chance to show what you know.

1. Read the label above each plant below.

2. Color the insects at the bottom of the page.

3. Cut out the insects.

4. Paste each insect on the plant where it belongs.

Complete Metamorphosis   **Incomplete Metamorphosis**

Name _____

Symphony Instruments

Have you ever listened to the sweet strings of symphony violins? Perhaps you have heard the light melody of the flutes. Or maybe you have heard the ping of harp strings. The musicians in the orchestra are seated in special places to make the music sound just right. The diagram below shows where musicians normally sit in an orchestra.

Directions: Study the diagram below and answer the questions on page 35.

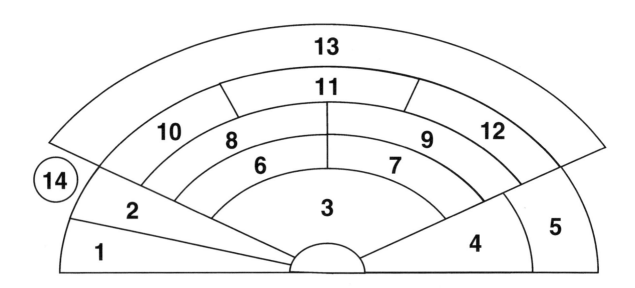

STRINGS	WOODWINDS	BRASS
1. First Violins	6. Flutes	10. Horns
2. Second Violins	7. Oboes	11. Trumpets
3. Violas	8. Clarinets	12. Trombones / Tuba
4. Cellos	9. Bassoons	13. Percussion / Timpani
5. Double Basses		14. Harp

Name _____

Directions: Use the diagram on page 34 to complete the exercises below.

---

1. How many types of instruments are in the String section?

   _____

2. Oboes are in the _____ section.

3. Bassoons are in the _____ section.

4. Number 6 in the diagram stands for _____.
   This instrument is in the _____ section.

5. Who sits farther from the double basses, the trombones or the clarinets?

   _____

6. Who sits closer to the first violins, the horns or the double basses?

   _____

7. Does the conductor stand closer to the violas or the harp?

   _____

8. Is the harp closer to the horns or the tuba?

   _____

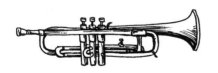

Name _____

Music Camp

Luther is packing for music camp. He is the best clarinet player in his school. He loves music, and he goes to music camp every year. Luther does all the things campers usually do, but he also gets to play his clarinet. As Luther packs, he is separating items into three groups.

Directions: Look at the three categories of items Luther is sorting. Look at the items. Color and cut out the items. Place each in the group where it belongs.

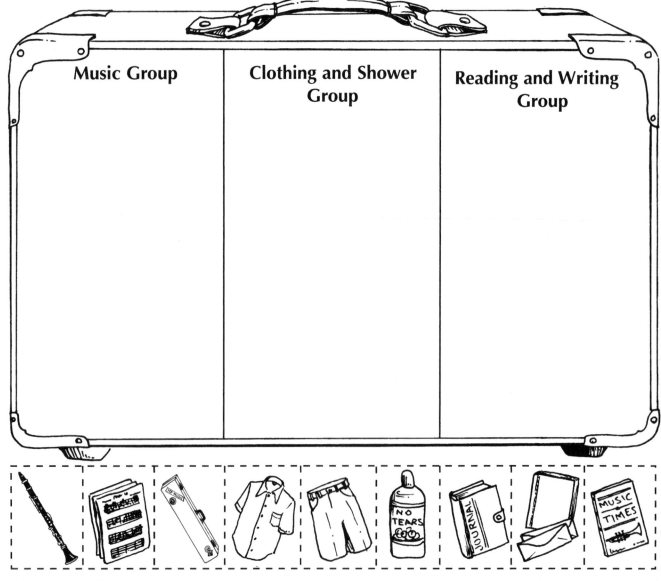

Music Group	Clothing and Shower Group	Reading and Writing Group

Name _____

Chapter Chooser

Directions: Use the table of contents to answer the questions on page 40.

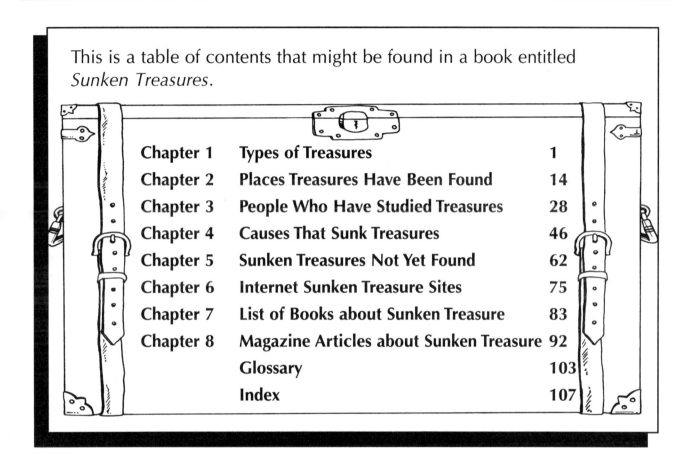

This is a table of contents that might be found in a book entitled *Sunken Treasures*.

1. Suki needs to find out how coins and jewelry from sunken treasure are alike and different. Which chapter will likely help her the most? Why?

   _____

   _____

2. Bill knows that an earthquake sank one city. He wants to know what sank other cities and their treasures. Which chapter will most likely help him? Why?

   _____

   _____

Name _____

> **Directions:** Use the table of contents found on page 39 to help complete these
> questions.

---

3. Which chapter is the longest? _____.

4. Which chapter is sixteen pages long? _____.

5. Which two chapters are the same length? _____.

6. Chapter 7 ends on page _____.

7. Danika heard about a treasure that sank on a ship during the 1700s.
   No one has found the treasure yet. Danika wants to learn more about
   it. Which chapter will most likely help? _____.

8. José is writing a report about sunken treasures. He must read at least
   two books and at least three magazine articles. The two chapters that
   will likely give him the most help are chapters

   _____ and _____.

9. Ling wants to read about divers who have worked with sunken treasure. The chapter that will likely give her the most help is chapter

   _____.

10. Taisha has found a word in chapter 6 that she does not understand.
    She wants to know what the word means. Where should she look?

    _____

Name _____

Right Back at You!

Perhaps you have heard that many types of bats have very small eyes and do not see well. Still, as they swoop through the night, they do not bump into objects and are able to find food, even though they cannot see their prey. How is this possible? Echolocation!

You might recognize the beginning of the word echolocation as echo, and you might recognize the last part of the word as location. This gives you clues about how echolocation works. The bat sends out sounds. The sounds bounce off objects and return to the bat. Echolocation not only tells the bat that objects are nearby. It also tells the bat just how far away the objects are.

Bats are not the only creatures who use echolocation. Porpoises and some types of whales and birds use it as well.

Directions: Answer the questions about the passage you have just read.

1. Why did the author most likely write this passage? Circle one reason below and tell why you made your choice.

- to convince you to visit bats?
- to tell you a funny story about bats?
- to give you information about bats?
- to describe feelings about bats?

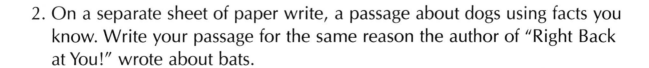

_____

_____

2. On a separate sheet of paper write, a passage about dogs using facts you know. Write your passage for the same reason the author of "Right Back at You!" wrote about bats.

Name _____

Mr. Wong's Assignment

Directions: Read all of Mr. Wong's assignment sheet. Follow the directions.
Write what lesson you learned from the assignment. Use complete sentences.

Directions: Read the entire sheet before you begin writing.

Name: _____

1. Circle the numeral 1.

2. Underline the word numeral in direction 1.

3. Draw a star in the space below this sentence.

4. Draw a circle at the end of this sentence.

5. Underline this sentence.

6. Draw a triangle in the space below this sentence.

7. Draw a square at the end of this sentence.

8. Circle your name.

9. Draw a triangle around the period in this sentence.

10. Pay no attention to numbers 1–9. Only write your name at the top
    of the page above the directions.

_____

_____

_____

_____

_____

_____

_____

Name _____

Map Symbols

Directions: Use the map key below for maps A, B, and C here and on page 44. Read the directions for each map. Draw symbols where they belong.

Many maps use symbols, or pictures, to show where things are located. Below is a good example of a map key for maps A, B, and C.

school	road	railroad tracks	store
house	bridge	lake	park

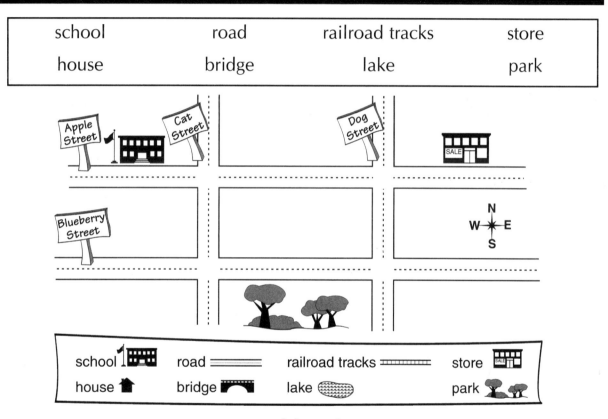

Map A

1. There is a house on Blueberry Street. The house is west of the park. Draw the house symbol where it belongs.

2. There is a lake between Cat and Dog Streets. The lake is north of the park. Draw the lake symbol where it belongs.

3. There is a bridge that children and their parents can cross to walk from school to the store. Draw the bridge symbol where it belongs.

Directions: Use the map key on page 43 to complete the activities below.

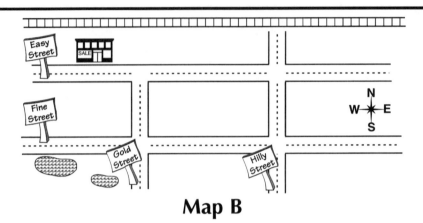

Map B

1. A bridge connects the two lakes. Draw the bridge symbol.

2. There is a park to the south of the railroad tracks. The park is east of Hilly Street. Draw the symbol for the park where it belongs.

3. The school is on Fine Street. It is east of Gold Street and west of Hilly Street. Draw the symbol for the school where it belongs.

Map C

Draw a map of your own. Use the symbols in the map key on page 43.

1. Draw the same streets as you see them in Map A. Label each street.

2. The school on this map is between Cat Street and Dog Street. It is north of Apple Street.

3. The park is north of Apple Street and east of Dog Street.

4. There is a bridge that connects Apple Street and Blueberry Street. The bridge is west of Cat Street.

5. There is a lake to the east of Dog Street and south of Blueberry Street.

Name _____

Stamp Art

Directions: Read about some stamps and post cards. Then complete page 46.

Over the years, the United States Postal Service has issued many stamps and post cards. Each has its own story and an original illustration to match. Here are descriptions of a few stamps issued between 1997 and 2001.

In 1997, the Postal Service issued post cards that showed the glory of the Golden Gate Bridge in San Francisco. One showed the Golden Gate Bridge during sunlight. The bridge is an orange-gold color and crosses the entire card. The letters USA are in the upper right corner of the card. The number twenty appears to the right of the letters. This tells how much the card cost in 1997. The background behind the bridge is a lovely light blue. A green hill rises to the left behind the bridge.

The theme of one 1998 stamp was winter sports. It was created to show the strength and speed of an alpine skier on a very steep slope. The stamp showed a skier on a snowy slope. The skis were black, and the background was purple. In the lower right corner appeared the letters USA with the number thirty-two below them.

Bugs looked as if they were crawling and flying across stamps in 1999. One stamp showed an orange and black butterfly. The number thirty-three appeared in the top left corner of the stamp. Above the number appeared the letters USA.

In 2000, a snake coiled across a stamp. The snake looked happy. Green leaves appeared around it. The snake was light orange, green, and blue. The stamp had a purple background. In large letters, the number thirty-four appeared in the lower right corner. The letters USA appeared above the number four. The bottoms of the letters faced the outside right edge. In the top of the right-hand corner, you could see the phrase HAPPY NEW YEAR! all in capital letters. This stamp was created in honor of the Chinese Lunar New Year during the Year of the Snake.

Name _____

Directions: Draw and color each stamp or post card. Use the dates below each box and the descriptions found on page 45 to help you.

1997
_____

1998
_____

1999
_____

2000
_____

Name _____

Coaching Your Systems

Directions: Read these facts about the brain. Use what you learn to complete activities on pages 47 and 48.

Have you ever watched a coach during a ball game? The coach tells players where to go and what to do as things are happening in the game. Your brain is like your coach. Information from your five senses—touch, smell, hearing, taste, sight—races to your brain. Your brain sorts out the information and lets your body know what to do.

Your brain has three main parts, the medulla, cerebrum, and cerebellum. Perhaps you have heard someone talk about "gray matter" while discussing intelligence. This refers to the cerebrum. The cerebrum is large, and its outside layer is gray and looks wrinkled. The cerebrum, the cerebral cortex, springs to work when you are doing something that requires a good deal of thought. If you are taking a test, talking to a friend, or reading directions to put together a new bicycle, your cerebrum is busy.

As you try to keep your balance on your bicycle, it is your cerebellum that is called to work. The cerebellum is in control of balance and coordination. It is much smaller than the cerebrum.

The medulla is your brain stem. It is the lowest part of your brain. The medulla controls breathing and heart rate.

The next time you put together a bicycle, hop on, and gasp for breath after riding up a hill, you will know that all the parts of your brain have been very busy.

1. If you were walking a tightrope, which part of your brain would help you keep your balance?

_____

Directions: Use the facts you read on page 47 to help complete these activities.

2. You have just run a great distance, and you are trying to catch your breath. Which part of your brain will help you?

_____

3. Suppose that you want to buy a new video game. You are counting up your savings to see how much more money you will need to save. Which part of your brain is helping you with the math?

_____

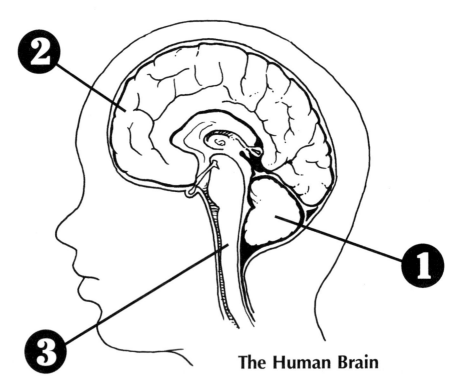

The Human Brain

Look at the diagram above. Name the parts of the brain.

4. _____

5. _____

6. _____

Name _____

Food Pyramid

Directions: Study the food pyramid. Then write the number of each food in the list below in the correct section of the pyramid.

What foods should you eat to stay healthy? The food pyramid shows how many servings children should have in each food group each day.

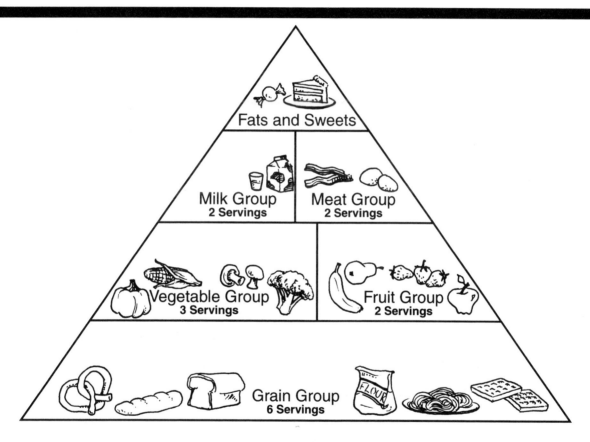

1. orange

2. yogurt

3. cookie

4. carrot

5. chicken leg

6. pancake

7. breakfast cereal

8. milk

9. potato

10. roast beef

11. cupcake

12. cheese

Name _____

On the Richter Scale

Directions: Study this information about earthquakes and the Richter Scale.

The Richter Scale was developed by Charles Richter. It compares the size of earthquakes. The scale below shows how big or serious an earthquake is. This is the earthquake's magnitude.

Chart A—Annual Average Occurrence and Magnitude of Earthquakes

Magnitude	Annual Average	Description
3.0–less	9,000 daily	People do not usually feel the earthquake.
3.1–3.9	49,000—estimated	People can feel the earthquake. It causes little damage.
4.0–4.9	6,200—estimated	People can feel the earthquake. It causes little damage.
5.0–5.9	800	Buildings can be damaged.
6.0–6.9	120	It can cause a great deal of damage in a large area.
7.0–7.9	18	It can cause a great deal of damage in a large area.
8.0 and greater	1	It can cause very serious damage and possibly loss of life across very large areas.

Chart B—How Often Earthquakes Happened Since 1995

Magnitude	1995	1996	1997	1998	1999	2000
3.0–less	6328	4870	6204	7332	7017	7961
3.1–3.9	5002	4869	4467	5945	5521	4741
4.0–4.9	8140	8794	7938	7303	7042	8114
5.0–5.9	1327	1223	1118	979	1106	1318
6.0–6.9	185	160	125	113	123	157
7.0–7.9	22	21	20	14	23	14
8.0 and greater	3	1	0	2	0	4
Total	21,007	19,938	19,872	21,688	22,711	22,309

Name _____

Directions: Answer these questions about earthquakes using the information on page 50.

1. What is the annual average number of earthquakes that measure 5.0–5.9 on the Richter Scale? What chart did you use to find your answer?

    _____

    _____

2. According to Chart B, which magnitude earthquake has occurred most often since 1995?

    _____

    _____

3. How might you describe an earthquake that measures 6.0–6.9 on the Richter Scale?

    _____

    _____

4. Which year did the most 8.0–greater earthquakes occur? What chart did you use to find your answer?

    _____

    _____

5. Which magnitude earthquake is the most common on an annual basis? Which is the least common? How do you know?

    _____

    _____

Name _____

 # Charting Hurricanes

This chart shows information about hurricanes that occurred in the United States.
Names and Years of Hurricanes

Hurricane Name	Year Hurricane Struck	States Hurricanes Struck
Galveston Storm	1900	Texas
Audrey	1957	Louisiana
Alicia	1983	Texas
Gilbert	1988	Florida
Hugo	1989	South Carolina
Fran	1996	North Carolina

Directions: Read the chart above and answer the questions below.

1. Name two hurricanes that struck in the same state. When did they occur?

   _____

2. Is this chart arranged by alphabetical order of storm names or by date? How do you know?

   _____

3. Two hurricanes struck one year apart. Name the hurricanes and the years.

   _____

4. One of the storms that is shown happened before hurricanes were given peoples' names. Which hurricane is that?

   _____

5. Name the hurricane that occurred at the beginning of a new century?

   _____

Name _____

Dance School

Jack's family owns a dance school. These pie graphs show information about the classes offered at the school and the students who take those classes.

Directions: Use the pie graphs to answer the questions below.

Chart A: Types of Dance Classes

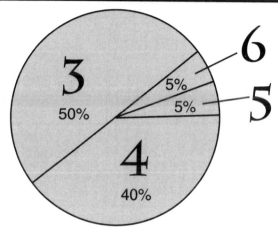

Chart B: Number of Students from Each Grade Taking Classes

1. Which type of dance class do most students take? Which chart did you use to answer this question? Why?

   _____

2. Are there more fifth graders than fourth graders taking dance classes? Which chart did you use to answer this question? Why?

   _____

3. Name the two kinds of dance classes that have the same number of students.

   _____

4. Suppose the dance school can only offer two kinds of dance classes. Which two classes should the school choose? Why?

   _____

Name _____

Yum! It Came from Milk!

Many products come from milk. Some of them are healthier than others. The graphs below give information about cheese and ice cream produced in the United States.

Directions: Read each graph and answer the questions that follow.

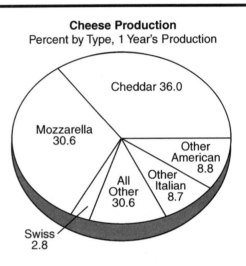

1. During what year was the greatest amount of regular ice cream produced? _____

2. During what year was the smallest amount of regular ice cream produced?

   _____

3. During what two years did the United States produce about the same amount of regular ice cream? _____

4. During what year did the United State produce more than 880 gallons (3,330 L), but less than 900 gallons (3,407 L)? _____

5. What was the total number of gallons produced during Year Four and Year Five? _____

6. What type of cheese was produced in the greatest amount?

   _____

7. What type of cheese was produced in the smallest amount?

   _____

Name _____

Latitude Attitude

Latitude is measured in degrees, but what does latitude measure? It measures how far north or south a place is from the equator. Latitude lines are imaginary lines. You will find them drawn on a map every twenty degrees north and south of the equator. Latitudes near the equator are very hot. The closer a place is to the equator, the warmer its climate. As you travel farther from the equator, the temperatures drop. The diagram below shows the equator and latitudes north and south of the equator.

Directions: Study the diagram and answer the questions.

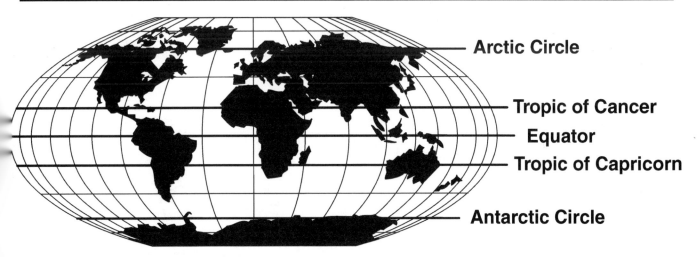

1. Which is probably colder, the Arctic Circle or the Tropic of Cancer? How do you know? _____

   _____

2. Is the climate of the Tropic of Cancer likely the same as the climate of the Tropic of Capricorn? How do you know? _____

   _____

3. Of all the areas on the diagram, which is the hottest? _____

   _____

Name _____

Time Zones

When it is daytime in the United States, is it daytime all around the world? No. When it is daytime in the United States, the United States is facing the sun. Days and nights come about as the earth rotates on its axis. When it is daytime in the United States it is nighttime in Asia, for example, because Asia is the side of the earth facing away from the sun.

Even in the United States, the time is not the same in every state. The United States is divided into different time zones. The time can differ by as much as a few hours from state to state. And times in time zones can change with daylight savings time.

Directions: This map shows time zones in the United States. Study the map and answer the questions that follow.

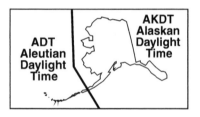

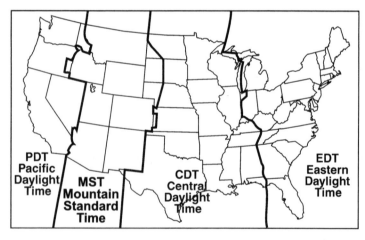

1. Name two states that are in the Mountain Standard time zone on this map. _____

2. If the time is 9:00 p.m. in New York, what time is it in Texas? _____

3. If the time is 4:00 p.m. in California, what time is it in Pennsylvania?

_____

4. Florida is in the _____ time zone.

5. In what time zone is your state? _____

Return to Sender

Marisol ordered a backpack online. This was exactly the backpack she needed for school. When the backpack arrived, Marisol opened the box. The zipper was broken!

Marisol sent an e-mail to the company, but was told the company did not give refunds. She decided to write a letter to the president of the company and express her concerns.

Directions: Read the two letters that Marisol wrote. In the space below, tell which letter you think she should send. Give specific reasons why.

Dear Ms. Yuen:

I am so angry! I bought a backpack from your company. I just got it in the mail and the zipper is broken. I can't believe that your company would send out something like this. Who do you think you are? If you don't send me a refund right away, I'm taking you to court.

Marisol Rodriguez

Dear Ms. Yuen:

I recently received a backpack from your company. I was disappointed to see that the zipper was broken. I have ordered from you before and everything has always been fine. Would you please send me a refund or a new backpack? School is starting soon and I would like to have it.

Thank you,

Marisol Rodriguez

_____

_____

_____

_____

_____

_____

Name _____

Ellis Island

Thousands of immigrants arrived each day at Ellis Island in New York. This was one of the reception centers set up by the United States government. The immigrants arrived with high hopes. Many had a great deal to offer the United States. However, not all those who came through Ellis Island were allowed to stay in this country.

Immigrants had forms to fill out, questions to answer, and medical examinations to face. They waited for many hours in the Great Hall to hear their names called. Many had spent months in poor conditions on ships to come to the United States to make a better life. They had spent their savings to make the trip. Even after this, some were turned away.

Directions: Below, and on page 63, you will see the questions that immigrants had to answer when they arrived at Ellis Island. Do not answer any of the questions yourself. Instead, explain why you think each question was included. When you have finished, imagine that you are an immigrant. Write a journal entry to tell how you are feeling as you wait for your name to be called.

1. What is your name?

   _____

   _____

2. From what area are you arriving?

   _____

   _____

3. Who paid your fare?

   _____

   _____

Directions: Use the information on page 62 to complete the activities below.

---

4. Have you ever been hospitalized for insanity (put in the hospital because you were not of sound mind)?

   _____

5. Have you ever been imprisoned (put in jail)?

   _____

6. Are you an anarchist (against the government)?

   _____

7. Are you in possession of at least $50.00?

   _____

8. To what city are you traveling?

   _____

9. Do you have a ticket to this city?

   _____

10. Do you have a job waiting for you?

   _____

Your Journal Entry

_____

_____

_____

_____

_____

_____

Fact or Opinion

What Do You Think?

Name _____

Facts are statements that can be proven true or false. Opinions are statements that express how someone thinks or feels about a situation.

Directions: Write Fact or Opinion to tell whether each sentence below tells a fact or an opinion.

_____ 1. France is the most beautiful country in the world.

_____ 2. The population of California is larger than the population of Rhode Island.

_____ 3. People on farms work harder than people in factories.

_____ 4. Teachers in Maine are better than teachers in New Mexico.

_____ 5. Idaho produces more potatoes than any other state in the United States.

_____ 6. People need food and water to survive.

_____ 7. José believes that Oregon is the best place to live.

_____ 8. A system of roads crisscrosses the United States.

_____ 9. Robert Fulton invented the steam engine.

_____ 10. The most interesting books are read in third grade.

_____ 11. Florida is a wonderful state.

_____ 12. Transportation in the United States includes automobiles, trains, and airplanes.

13. Write a statement of fact.

_____

14. Write a statement that expresses your opinion about something.

_____

Name _____

The Statue of Liberty

Directions: Use the passage and chart below to answer the questions on page 74. When answering, think about what you read and what you already know.

As immigrants to the United States sailed into New York, they gazed up at Lady Liberty and the torch she holds high. France gave this famous statue to the United States. Original plans were made to deliver the Statue of Liberty in 1876 to celebrate the one-hundred-year anniversary of a very important United States event.

It was agreed that the French would build the statue. The United States was to provide the pedestal, or stand. Both France and the United States had problems raising funds, so Lady Liberty celebrated her one-hundredth birthday on October 28, 1986, ten years later than planned.

Getting the statue to the United States was no easy task. It had to be taken apart and packed into two hundred and fourteen crates. There were more than three hundred fifty pieces in all. It took one-third of a year to put all the pieces of the statue together on the pedestal.

Statue of Liberty Dimensions—Standard and Metric

Heel to top of head	111'1"	33.86 m
Length of hand	16'5"	5.00 m
Index finger	8'0"	2.44 m
Distance across the eye	2'6"	.76 m
Length of nose	4'6"	1.37 m
Width of mouth	3'0"	.91 m

Name _____

Directions: Use the information on page 73 to help complete these questions.

1. The passage tells you that the statue was given to the United States by France in 1876 to celebrate the 100-year anniversary of a very important U.S. event. What was this event? (Hint: Think about the year.)

   _____

2. The passage tells you that plans were made to deliver the statue in 1876. Was the statue delivered during this year? How do you know?

   _____

   _____

3. How many months did it take to put the statue together? How do you know?

   _____

4. The length of Lady Liberty's _____ is about half the length of her hand.

5. The length of Lady Liberty's _____ is about half the length of her index finger.

6. Which is greater, the width of Lady Liberty's mouth or the length of her nose?

   _____

7. What is the distance from Lady Liberty's heel to the top of her head?

   _____

Name _____

How Does That Work?

Rube Goldberg loved to draw. He was intelligent and, though he studied engineering in college, he continued to draw. After college, he went to work as an artist. He found a job as an office helper at a newspaper, and he kept sending his drawings and cartoons to the editor. He wanted to see them published in the newspaper. He succeeded!

Goldberg was so successful that his drawings appeared in newspapers all over the world. Many of Goldberg's drawings showed inventions he had created. The drawings showed ways to cause great results through simple efforts. You can see an illustration similar to Goldberg's invention drawings below.

Directions: Use the information on this page to help complete the questions.

The pillow falling to the ground is a cause and an effect.

1. It is the effect of

_____

2. It is the cause of

_____

Name _____

Directions: Draw your own Rube Goldberg-style invention. Show at least three causes and their effects in your picture.

Directions: Use the information from page 78 to complete these activities.

---

1. The invention of the telephone caused many changes in the world. Why was the invention of the telephone important? What are some of the results of the invention of the telephone? (Hint: You won't find all the information in the passage.)

   _____

   _____

   _____

   _____

   _____

2. Review the details in the passage as you fill in the missing information in the timeline below.

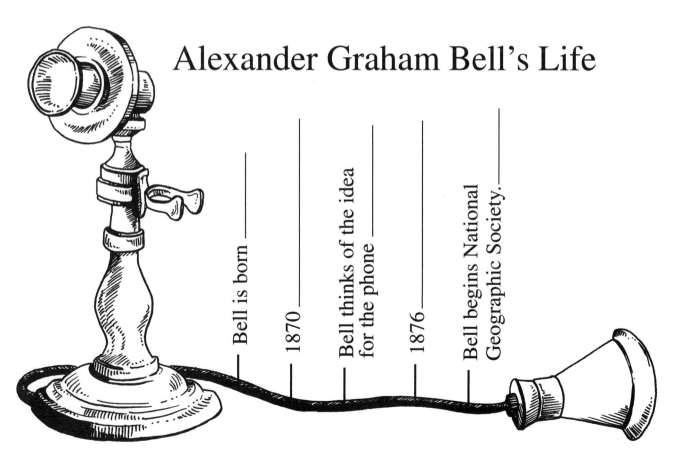

Alexander Graham Bell's Life

Bell is born — 1870 — Bell thinks of the idea for the phone — 1876 — Bell begins National Geographic Society.

The Great Lakes

Have you ever wondered how the Great Lakes came to be? What caused so many large lakes to be in one area of the United States? The same elements came together to cause the Finger Lakes in New York, Lake Superior, Lake Michigan, Lake Huron, Lake Erie, and Lake Ontario.

Thousands of years ago, glaciers—huge masses of slowly moving ice—covered the earth. More and more snow fell. Temperatures grew colder. Glaciers grew larger and larger.

The movement of glaciers pulled up huge amounts of soil and rocks. These were shoved ahead and to the sides of the glaciers.

Warming temperatures caused the glaciers to melt. The glaciers had taken up space. The soil and rocks pulled up and shoved along by the glaciers had taken up space. When the glaciers melted, there were huge holes.

Water from melting glaciers and from rain filled these huge holes. They were no longer holes. They were lakes!

Directions: List two causes and effects from the passage in the space below. Draw an illustration to show each cause and effect.

1. Cause: _____

_____

Effect: _____

_____

Drawing:

Name _____

Directions: Use the information on page 80 to write a cause and effect statement. Then illustrate the statement. For number 3, create your own cause and effect statements on another topic. Draw an illustration to show the cause and effect.

2. Cause: _____

_____

Effect: _____

_____

Drawing:

3. Cause: _____

_____

Effect: _____

_____

Drawing:

Name _____

Preparing for an Eruption

Directions: Think about the information as you circle each correct answer.

People in the city of Rabaul live in a huge volcanic crater. Because of this, they know they need an escape plan in case of an eruption.

In the fall of 1994, people began to notice signs of an eruption. The older residents of Rabaul recognized the signs. Birds flew away from their nests, the ground shook in an up-and-down motion rather than side-to-side, and sea snakes slithered out of the ocean. Dogs barked and smelled the ground and pawed at it.

On the day of the eruption, earthquakes shook Rabaul. More than 50,000 people left the area. The volcano erupted. Some said that five vents erupted at one time. Volcanic ash filled the sky.

When the smoke cleared, about three-fourths of the houses on the island had been flattened. The island suffered greatly, but only a very few people lost their lives. The planning had paid off.

1. When did the people begin to notice signs of a coming volcanic eruption?

   a. January   b. March

   c. July   d. October

2. What was the clue from the story that helped answer question one?

   _____

3. How did they know that it was time to take action?

   a. They lived in a volcanic crater.   b. Unusual things happened.

   c. Many houses collapsed.   d. People owned dogs.

4. What was the clue from the story that helped answer question three?

   _____

Name _____

Artists and Their Art

Directions: Read about these six world-famous artists. Use the information to complete the activities on page 84. Then draw and color a picture in your own special style.

Pierre-Auguste Renoir's early career was that of a shoemaker and dress tailor. He believed in working with his hands. Renoir is known for his portraits of women and groups of people. He had a true talent for using light and color.

Henri de Toulouse-Lautrec liked to paint many subjects. Among his favorites were houses. He painted a portrait of Vincent Van Gogh.

Vincent Van Gogh painted in a style similar to that of Toulouse-Latrec. One of his most famous paintings is *The Starry Night*. It shows beautiful stars against a blue-black sky.

Claude Monet had many gardens around his home. While he painted many subjects, his gardens are some of those for which he is most famous.

Salvador Dali painted in a more unusual style. The items you could see in Dali's works were things you might see every day, but Dali changed them. He made them look unusual. For example, one of his paintings shows clocks that are melting.

Andy Warhol's artwork was even more unusual than Dali's. His style was called Pop Art. Many of his pieces showed things that people see every day, like soup cans and money.

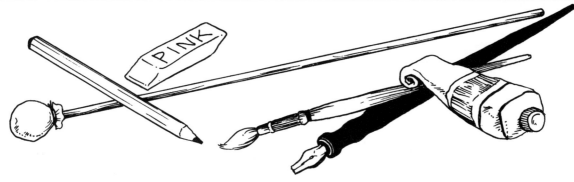

Directions: Use information from page 83 to help draw pictures in the artists' style. Then on a separate sheet, draw a picture using your own special style.

Renoir

Toulouse-Latrec

Van Gogh

Monet

Dali

Warhol

Name _____

Preparing for an Earthquake

Directions: Read the information on earthquakes and earthquake plans. Use the facts to complete the activities on page 86.

Until scientists can determine when earthquakes will happen, people can take action to protect themselves. People can learn from past earthquakes and prepare for them. In 1994, an earthquake struck in Northridge, California. A fault deep below the surface caused the earthquake. Scientists did not even know that the fault existed.

This experience gave people the message that they should be prepared. It is possible for earthquakes to occur anywhere throughout the world.

How do people prepare for earthquakes? The American Red Cross has some good advice for people living in areas where earthquakes do occur. This can help save lives.

Have a Home Earthquake Plan. This plan gives a place in every room where people will be the safest, under a table or against an inside wall away from things that could fall.

Practice DROP, COVER, and HOLD ON! Here's how: get to a safe place. Cover your eyes with your arm. Wait until you know it is safe to move.

Keep your home safe. Put strong latches on cabinets. Strap down the water heater and tall bookcases. Keep a supply kit in your home and car. Include things such as a first aid kit, fresh water, canned food, a can opener, and a flashlight.

Everyone should be prepared in case an earthquake strikes close to home.

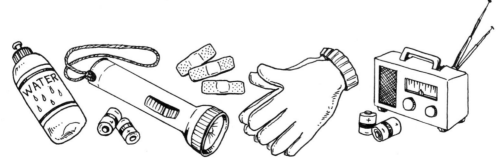

Name _____

> **Directions:** Complete the activities below after reading page 85.

1. Finish the picture below, showing the main idea of the passage on page 85.

2. In each house, write one supporting detail of the main idea from the passage on page 85.

Name _____

Here Comes the Sun

Directions: Read the paragraph and answer the questions below.

It is possible that the ancient Mayan civilization was destroyed by drought. The civilization developed in a place where there were many periods of drought, times with little or no rain. The Mayan people lived in a very hot area where they needed the rainwater to live. The Mayan people built huge beautiful buildings, pyramids, which were temples to the stars and planets that they worshiped. One of the stars, the sun, with all of its heat, may have contributed to the ending of this ancient people by drying up the little bit of water they had for growing crops.

1. What is the main idea of this paragraph?

   _____

   _____

2. What are two supporting ideas from this paragraph?

   _____

   _____

   _____

3. What would be another good title for this paragraph?

   _____

Name _____

A Trip Through the Ages

Directions: Use the timeline and map below to answer the questions on this page and on page 89.

Pre-Cambrian Era	Paleozoic Era	Mezazoic Era	Mesozoic Era
◆ Small creatures swim in the ocean. ◆ Creatures have no backbones.	◆ Fish swim in the ocean. ◆ Some animals have backbones. ◆ There is only one continent on Earth. It is Pangaea.	◆ Dinosaurs rule. ◆ Pangaea has separated into seven continents.	◆ Dinosaurs are extinct. ◆ There are many mammals on Earth, including humans.
4.5 Billion to 600 Million years ago	**600 to 230 Million years ago**	**230 to 70 Million years ago**	**70 Million years ago to the Present**

1. According to the timeline, did the Mesozoic Era begin before or after the Pre-Cambrian Era?

    _____

2. Which era was later, the Paleozoic Era or the Cenozoic Era?

    _____

3. What era are you living in right now?

    _____

4. Study the map below and the timeline above. Could this map have been correct during the Paleozoic Era? Why or why not?

    _____
    _____
    _____
    _____
    _____
    _____

Directions: Answer the questions about Earth's history using the timeline on page 88 and the information provided below.

5. Look at this picture. Is it possible that this picture is showing the Pre-Cambrian Era? Why or why not?

    _____

    _____

6. Study the picture below. Is it possible that this picture is showing the Cenozoic Era? Why or why not?

    _____

    _____

7. Draw a timeline that shows important events in your life, such as the day you were born. Include at least four dates and one phrase or sentence describing each date. If necessary, use a separate sheet of paper.

Name _____

Thomas Jefferson

Thomas Jefferson accomplished many great things. He is probably best known as the main author of the Declaration of Independence and the third president of the United States. Jefferson was born in 1743. He graduated from the College of William and Mary in 1762 and studied to become a lawyer.

He entered politics in 1769 and became governor of Virginia in 1779. Jefferson went on to become a member of the Continental Congress in 1783 and the minister to France in 1784. By 1790, he had become Secretary of State, and in 1797, he became vice president. He missed becoming President by only three votes. The law at that time made him vice president. In 1801, he became President of the United States.

Jefferson was only thirty-three years old when he helped write the Declaration of Independence. He stood behind every word during his entire political career. He worked to see that the principles of the Declaration of Independence became reality.

Jefferson served as United States President from 1801 to 1809. He continued to work for his principles until he passed away in 1826.

Directions: Use information from the passage above to create a timeline of Thomas Jefferson's life. Include four years and the event from each one.

Name _____

Declaration of Independence

The United States worked hard to become a nation free from British rule. Richard Henry Lee brought a resolution before the Continental Congress. It said ". . . these United Colonies are, and of right ought to be, free and independent States."

A committee was appointed to write a formal statement of independence. Members of the committee included Thomas Jefferson, Robert Livingston, John Adams, Roger Sherman, and Benjamin Franklin. The committee members wanted Thomas Jefferson to write the Declaration of Independence because he was known for being such a fine statesman and writer.

Directions: Use the timeline of historic events and the information above to help answer the questions below.

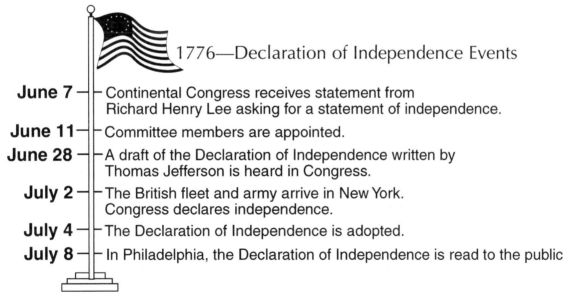

1776—Declaration of Independence Events

June 7 — Continental Congress receives statement from Richard Henry Lee asking for a statement of independence.

June 11 — Committee members are appointed.

June 28 — A draft of the Declaration of Independence written by Thomas Jefferson is heard in Congress.

July 2 — The British fleet and army arrive in New York. Congress declares independence.

July 4 — The Declaration of Independence is adopted.

July 8 — In Philadelphia, the Declaration of Independence is read to the public

1. Which of these events happened first?

   a. Thomas Jefferson wrote the Declaration of Independence.

   b. The Continental Congress received a statement from Richard Henry Lee.

   c. John Adams was named to the committee to draft the Declaration of Independence.

   d. The British fleet arrived in New York.

Directions: Use information from page 91 to complete these questions.

2. Which event happened during the last week of June?

    a. The Declaration of Independence was adopted.

    b. The British fleet and army arrived in New York.

    c. The Declaration of Independence was read to the public.

    d. A draft of the Declaration of Independence was heard in Congress.

3. Which event happened during the second week of July?

    a. The Declaration of Independence was adopted.

    b. The British fleet and army arrived in New York.

    c. The Declaration of Independence was read to the public.

    d. A draft of the Declaration of Independence was heard in Congress.

4. When were committee members appointed?

    a. Before the British fleet and army arrived in New York

    b. After the British fleet and army arrived in New York

    c. At the same time as the British fleet and army arrived in New York

    d. The timeline does not give information about committee members.

5. Which event happened four days after Thomas Jefferson's draft of the Declaration of Independence was heard in Congress?

    a. The Declaration of Independence was read to the public.

    b. Congress adopted the Declaration of Independence.

    c. The British army and fleet arrived in New York.

    d. Committee members were appointed.

Name _____

Ms. Domingo's Research Hunt

Ms. Domingo gave her students an Internet treasure hunt assignment. See how you do with the treasure hunt.

Directions: Look at the list of online resources the students can use to complete their treasure hunt. Choose the best resource for each task on pages 95 and 96. Write the item number next to the resource in the computer screen.

1. Omar has just written a letter to his grandmother. He needs one more piece of information before he can mail it. Look at Omar's envelope. Then choose the Internet link that could show Omar the information he needs.

_____

2. Felipe wants to use the word distress in a report. Where can he find the exact meaning of the word?

_____

Directions: Look at the list of online resources found on page 95. Write the item number next to the resource in the computer screen.

---

3. Annette wants to find all the pages in her book that give information about tigers. What resource will help her the most?

    _____

4. Tang wants to call her friend, but she does not know the number to dial. Where should she look?

    _____

5. Rodrigo is looking for a book that will give him the most help with a report about planets. What part of each book will help him decide whether to use it or not?

    _____

6. Tran wants to walk to her friend's house, but she is not exactly sure how to get there. Which resource will help her the most?

    _____

7. Bill has written this sentence in a report: *He felt okay.* Bill's teacher has asked him to list three words he might use in place of *okay.* Which resource will help him the most?

    _____

8. Keisha must answer the following question to complete her assignment. Which resource will help her the most? *Which country is closer to France, Poland or Spain?*

    _____

Name _____

City Beneath the Sea

Stories and reports from long ago tell of a beautiful city in Egypt. Egyptians called it *City at the Mouth of the Sea*. Ancient history tells that this city and nearby lands disappeared about 1,200 years ago.

As scientists studied the area, they came to believe that there had been a huge earthquake and tidal wave that sent the city beneath the Mediterranean Sea. In the year 2000, scientists found the city of Harakleion, which means Hercules.

Scientists found gigantic statues and hieroglyphics, a very old form of writing. But these were only two of the treasures hiding beneath the sea. They found sunken ships, jewelry, and gold coins as well. At the end of their search, researchers uncovered massive amounts of artifacts. One Egyptian official said that history was being reinvented at the hands of the people working with the sunken city and all its treasures.

Directions: Answer the questions using the information above.

1. What does Harakleion mean?

    a. Hieroglyphics   c. Hercules

    c. History   d. Highlight

2. In approximately what year did the city beneath the sea disappear?

    a. 400   b. 600

    c. 800   d. 1000

3. What did Egyptians call the sunken city?

    a. Golden City   b. City from the Earthquake

    c. Statue City   d. City at the Mouth of the Sea

4. Which of these were not found in the sunken city?

    a. gold   b. statues

    c. airplanes   d. ships

Name _____

Louisiana Purchase

Directions: Use the passage and the map below as you answer the questions on page 99 about the Louisiana Purchase.

In 1803, the United States entered into a treaty and bought a large amount of land from France. This land ran from Louisiana all the way up to the Rocky Mountains. The United States paid about 60 million francs, which is French money. That was about $15 million in American money.

President Thomas Jefferson was thrilled about gaining this land. Gaining land through a purchase was very different from gaining land through war. This was a positive step in American history.

When the Unites States gained Louisiana, it also acquired New Orleans. This gave the United States entry into the Mississippi River. One benefit of this was that farmers could more easily send their products to those waiting in far away markets. Before the Louisiana Purchase, Spain had controlled this area. Spain had been given this right by France.

With the Louisiana Purchase, the United States doubled its size.

Louisiana Purchase

Name _____

Directions: Use the passage and map found on page 98 as you answer the
questions about the Louisiana Purchase below.

---

1. List three reasons that explain why the Louisiana Purchase was good
   for the United States.

   _____

   _____

   _____

2. Who was President of the United States at the time of the Louisiana
   Purchase?

   _____

3. The Louisiana Purchase covered part or all of many of today's states.
   List four of the states.

   _____

   _____

   _____

   _____

4. _____ Country appears to the west of the Louisiana
   Purchase.

5. _____ Territory appears to the north of the Louisiana
   Purchase.

6. New Orleans is on the Gulf of _____.

Name _____

 # Weekly Assignments

Diego came down with the flu on Monday night, and his doctor told him to stay home from school for the rest of the week. She told him that he could do schoolwork on Thursday, but not to overdo it.

Directions: Read the notes Diego made about his assignments. Then answer the questions.

Monday

In class:
Finish poems.
Begin biography projects.

Homework:
Find Internet resources for projects.
Find quotes for biography.

Tuesday

In class:
Grammar pages—Subject-verb agreement, proofread poems

Homework:
Grammar pages—Capitalization

Wednesday

In class:
Meet in groups for biography projects.
Write invitation for talent show.

Homework:
Study for grammar test.

Thursday

No class, teacher in-service day

Friday

In class:
Field trip to the museum

Homework:
No homework!

1. Was Diego in class to finish his poem? How do you know?

   _____

2. Where and when will the class go on a field trip?

   _____

3. What kind of show needs an invitation?

   _____

4. Why isn't there class on Thursday?

   _____

Name _____

The Soldier's Lucky Coin

Directions: Read this story and use it to answer the questions on page 104.

George Dixon prepared to leave to fight in the United States Civil War. He was engaged to be married, and the woman he was engaged to gave him something special, a gold twenty-dollar coin, as a good luck token.

Dixon fought for his cause. During one battle, a bullet zipped toward his leg. Unbelievably, he was not harmed. Instead of hitting his leg, the bullet hit the gold coin he always carried in his pocket. The bullet bent the coin, but Dixon's leg was fine. The special gift from his sweetheart had kept him safe. Because of this, he had a special message written on the coin. The message listed the name of the battle and the date when the coin had saved his life.

Dixon left the battlefield to take command of a submarine. Dixon's submarine mysteriously sank and he was never seen again. What happened to Dixon? And what happened to the gold coin?

People heard about Dixon's story after the Civil War. Many believed that it was just a sweet story, a fable, or a bit of fiction. Others believed that it might be true.

Scientists have now found the remains of the H.L. Hunley, Dixon's submarine. When they first saw the submarine, it lay across the ocean floor. Archaeologists and other scientists searched through the submarine to learn more about it. They decided to bring the submarine up from the ocean floor so that others could see it.

One scientist reached down into a muddy area as preparations were made to show the submarine to the public. She felt ridges, the lines around the edge of a coin. A great thrill came over her. Carefully, she pulled out the coin. It was a very exciting moment when she realized what she was holding in her hand. It was a bent twenty-dollar coin with the same special message etched into it.

Name _____

> **Directions:** Use the story on page 103 to answer the questions below.

1. Was the story of the lucky soldier fact or fiction? How do you know?

   _____

   _____

2. Was the coin the scientist found the same coin George Dixon had lost? How do you know?

   _____

   _____

3. What is the main reason the author wrote this passage? Circle one of the answer choices.

   a. to describe feelings about lost coins

   b. to give you information about a lost coin

   c. to convince you to study lost coins

   d. to create a fun fiction passage

4. Explain why you chose the answer to number three.

   _____

   _____

5. Write a paragraph describing a time you found a lost item. Include a description of the item and the way you went about finding it.

   _____

   _____

   _____

   _____

   _____

   _____

Name _____

Samuel Morse

Directions: Use this information to answer the questions on page 106.

Have you ever watched someone tap a key and send a code for S.O.S.? Perhaps you have watched an old film and seen a ship about to sink. Perhaps someone was tapping wildly on a device, trying to send for help.

From where did this system of tapping out dashes and dots come? Who invented this electronic alphabet? Samuel Morse invented this system called Morse Code.

When Morse was young, he was an artist. People in New York knew his work well and liked it a great deal. Being well-known, Morse decided to run for office. He ran for the offices of New York mayor and Congressman, but he lost these political races.

In 1832, while Morse was sailing back to the United States from Europe, he thought of an electronic telegraph. This would help people communicate across great distances, even from ship to shore. He was anxious to put together his invention as quickly as possible. Interestingly, someone else had also thought of this same idea.

By 1835, he had put together his first telegraph, but it was only experimental. In 1844, he built a telegraph line from Baltimore to Washington, D.C. He later made his telegraph better, and in 1849, was granted a patent by the U.S. government. Within a few years, people communicated across 23,000 miles (37,007 km) of telegraph wire.

As a result of Samuel Morse's invention, trains ran more safely. Conductors could communicate about dangers or problems across great distances and ask for help. People in business could communicate more easily, which made it easier to sell their goods and services. Morse had changed communication forever.

Directions: Use page 105 to help answer the following questions.

1. The reason the author wrote this passage was most likely

    a. to tell a funny story about alphabets.

    b. to give information about an inventor.

    c. to convince you to communicate by telegraph.

    d. to describe personal feelings about communication.

2. Morse was successful in many areas. One area in which he tried and failed was

    a. painting.   b. communication.

    c. getting a patent.   d. running for politics.

3. Which did not result from Morse's invention?

    a. easier business communication

    b. safer train travel

    c. faster messages across the country

    d. more doctors in the United States

4. Where was Morse when he first thought of the telegraph?

    a. on a ship   b. on an airplane

    c. on a train   d. on a horse

5. What is something you might like to invent? Name the invention. Give a brief description. Explain what good your invention might do. Draw a picture of your invention on a separate sheet of paper.

    _____

    _____

    _____

    _____

    _____

Name _____

Native-American Biographies

Directions: Use the information found in the biographies below and on page 108 to complete the chart on page 108.

Many Native Americans have accomplished great things. You can read about some of these Native Americans here.

Wilma Mankiller

Wilma Mankiller was born in 1945. She is a Cherokee from Oklahoma. Mankiller lived in San Francisco for a long time before returning to Oklahoma. In San Francisco, she learned many skills that could help her as a chief. She became Principal Chief of the Cherokee Nation in 1985. She has worked hard for improved health care, civil rights, and many other important causes. Mankiller believes in an old Cherokee saying about being of good mind. She says today this is called "positive thinking."

Crazy Horse

A fierce warrior, Crazy Horse was known as a Lakota tribe member who would not give up. Born in 1849, Crazy Horse worked hard to keep the Native American way of life from disappearing. He did not want to lose the customs of his tribe. Most people say that Crazy Horse did not allow pictures to be taken of him, as this was against his belief. His image, though, is etched in stone on the Crazy Horse Memorial in South Dakota.

Wilma Mankiller	Crazy Horse	Chief Joseph	Red Cloud

Chief Joseph

Born in 1840, Chief Joseph was given a Native American name that meant *Thunder Rolling Down the Mountain*. Joseph became chief of the Nez Percé tribe. He was elected to this position after his father passed away. There were many attempts to force Joseph's group onto a small Idaho reservation. At first, Chief Joseph refused to go. Then he recognized that military force was too strong and would force him and his people to leave anyway. Joseph opposed war and so surrendered to the military. He only wanted peace for his people.

Red Cloud

Many believe that Red Cloud was one of the most important Lakota leaders of the nineteenth century. Born in 1822, Red Cloud became a great leader helping to hold and gain land for the Lakota. Red Cloud's work and the plans that he made to help his people were quite successful. As a result, the United States entered into a treaty that forced the U.S. to leave all of its forts in one area. The treaty also promised that the Lakota could keep a great amount of their land.

Name	Date Born	Tribe	Accomplishment

Name _____

Philo Farnsworth and Television

What would you say if someone asked who had invented the transmission, or sending, of television images? If you do not know the answer, you are not alone. Most people do not know that this was an invention of Philo Farnsworth. This is probably because a large company took Farnsworth's idea.

Farnsworth was born in a log cabin in 1906. When he was twelve, his family moved to a ranch. This put Farnsworth miles away from his school, and he rode his horse to get there.

Farnsworth was very interested in the electron and electricity. He asked one of his teachers to teach him outside of class and to let him sit in on a course for older students. The teacher agreed. The teacher later spoke of Farnsworth's intelligence and ability to communicate.

Farnsworth had the idea for sending television pictures when he was only fourteen. An article told of his invention when he was only twenty-two. How did it work? Moving images, or pictures, were broken into pinpoints of light. These pinpoints were changed into electrical impulses, or movements. Then the impulses were collected by the television set and changed back to light. People could see the images. A major magazine listed Farnsworth as one of the 100 great scientists and thinkers of the twentieth century.

What was the first image sent to a television? The dollar sign!

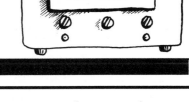

Directions: Use the information above to answer the questions here and on page 114. Circle the correct answer for each.

1. This passage could best be described as

    a. poetry.   b. play.

    c. biography.   d. fiction.

Name _____

Directions: Use the passage on page 113 to help complete these questions. Circle the correct answer to each question.

2. How old was Farnsworth when he first thought of the idea to send television images?

    a. 12   b. 14

    c. 20   d. 22

3. Which best describes Farnsworth?

    a. lazy   b. sad

    c. smart   d. bored

4. Draw a picture of a television. On the screen, show the first image sent to a TV.

5. Describe the process Philo Farnsworth used to send television pictures.

_____

_____

_____

_____

_____

_____

Name _____

Duke Ellington

When people hear Duke Ellington's name, they often think of "jazz.". When he was a child, he took piano lessons. But he wasn't excited about playing the piano. Instead, he wanted to be on the baseball field.

As Ellington grew older, he heard more and more piano players. He heard music in many styles. By the time he was in high school, he had developed a true love for the piano and had written his first piece of music. He began to play the piano at parties. He also played at clubs and dances. Ellington eventually had his own musical group.

Ellington decided to move to New York. He played in the famous Cotton Club. Soon, his music was broadcast over the radio. He was on the road to stardom. He quickly became one of the biggest names in jazz.

Directions: Each of these paragraphs needs a topic sentence. Write one for each. Then write a more exciting title for the passage.

1. First Paragraph—Topic Sentence

   _____

   _____

2. Second Paragraph—Topic Sentence

   _____

   _____

3. Third Paragraph—Topic Sentence

   _____

   _____

4. Exciting New Title

   _____

Name _____

Visiting the Big Apple

Directions: Read Delia's letter to her grandmother. Use the information to answer the questions on page 117.

Dear Grandma,

Guess where we went today? We went to see the Statue of Liberty. I couldn't believe how big it is. There's a huge torch in the statue's hand. I could see the statue as we sailed across to it. It looked big from the boat, but it was gigantic when I stood in front of it!

Yesterday, we took the elevator up to the top of the Empire State Building. We used telescopes to look out across the city. We were up so high!

Last night, we went to see a show on Broadway. The actors danced and sang. There was even an actress about my age in the show. I wonder if I could ever be in a Broadway show. I'd like to do that some day.

Of all the things we've done since we got here, visiting Ellis Island was my favorite. I know that our relatives came through there many years ago when they first came to the United States. It gave me goose bumps to stand in the same spot they probably stood! And I got to see all sorts of things people brought to our country.

Dad says it's time to go. We're going to Central Park today. I'm going to mail your letter in the hotel lobby. See you soon.

Love,

Delia

> **Directions:** Use the letter on page 116 to help answer the following questions.

1. What is the name of the city Delia is visiting?

    _____

2. What is a nickname for this city?

    _____

3. Name three places Delia visited.

    _____

4. Name one place Delia was getting ready to visit.

    _____

5. Where was Delia's favorite place to visit? Why?

    _____

    _____

6. Name one thing you learned about the city Delia visited.

    _____

    _____

7. What would Delia like to do one day?

    _____

8. From where was Delia going to mail Grandma's letter?

    _____

Name _____

Traveling the Internet Highway

Directions: Study these computer screens. They each have Web site listings. Computer A has sites for resources on the rain forest. Computer B shows a listing of sites that have information on the kelp forests. Use this to answer the questions found on page 119.

Computer A

Computer B

Name _____

Directions: Use the lists of Web sites found on computers A and B on page 118 to help answer the questions below. Copy the sites exactly.

---

1. Which site offers links to more kinds of information?

   _____

2. Through which site would you most likely find information about fish?

   _____

3. One site tells you who created the site. Which one? Who created the site?

   _____

4. One site shows you a link where you might learn about monkeys. Which site? Which link?

   _____

5. On the kelp forest site, which link would you use to find out what kind of kelp is in the Gulf of Mexico?

   _____

6. Suppose that you wanted to find out about the tallest building in the world. Which site gives a link you should try? What is the link?

   _____

7. What information would the site map link at the bottom of the rain forest site provide?

   _____

8. On which site would you find information about seaweed? Which link would you use?

   _____

9. Make up a Web site. Give it a title. Include at least four links.

   _____

Answer Key

Ants, Ants Everywhere!
(Compare and Contrast) 4–5
Answers will vary; sample answers appear below.
> **Fire Ants and Leaf Cutter Ants**: crawl, make mounds
> **Fire Ants**: bite, spread quickly
> **Leaf Cutter Ants**: help soil, carry leaf bits underground

Vote for Me (Compare and Contrast) 6
Answers will vary. Sample answers appear below.
> **Juan's poster**: neat, easy to read, states many specific ways to help
> **Samantha's poster**: rhymes, fun, only gives a couple of specific ways to help
> **Both posters**: give promises, promise class meetings, promise better lunchroom food

Volcanoes on Earth and Venus
(Compare and Contrast) 7
Answers will vary. Sample answers appear below.
> **Earth**: water on surface, volcanoes erupt in number of ways, cooler temperatures
> **Venus**: no water on surface, high clouds, very hot temperatures, eruptions of flat lava flows
> **Both**: clouds, thick atmosphere, almost same size, almost same mass, similar orbits

Kelp Forests and Our Ecology
(Compare and Contrast) 8–9
1. Lobster—because it is dark at the ocean's floor
2. Possible answer: Leafy treetops form the canopy of the rain forest; leafy parts of the kelp form the canopy of the kelp forest.
3. Possible answers:
   > **Rain forests**: on land, produce bananas
   > **Kelp forest**: in ocean, sea creatures, produce seafood
   > **Both**: important to ecology, keep animals safe, make home for many types of animals, produce food, have layers

Across the Great State of Texas
(Compare and Contrast) 10–11
1. Answers will vary. Sample answers appear below.
   > **Houston**: near the ocean, floods, Rockets play basketball
   > **Dallas**: snows, Mavericks play basketball
   > **Both**: in Texas, Interstate 45, hot during summer, sports arenas, Galveston beach

2. Answers will vary, but should include at least three correct entries in each section of the Venn diagram. The diagram should include labels in each section.
3. Answers will vary, but should match information in student's Venn diagram. Paragraph should include topic sentence; title should appear above paragraph.

Disaster! (Compare and Contrast) 12
Answers will vary. Possible comparisons appear below.
> **All**: carried passengers, had seats
> **Hindenburg and airplane**: both flew
> **Hindenburg and Titanic**: met with disaster, Hindenburg flew; Titanic sailed. Hindenburg was larger than an airplane.

The Underground Railroad
(Compare and Contrast) 13–14
Answers will vary. Sample answers appear below.
> **Underground Railroad**: helped slaves escape, people traveled in hiding, traveled at night
> **Railroad Trains**: traveled day and night, traveled on tracks
> **Both**: had conductors, passengers, stations, helped people move from place to place, great distances

Sending It Your Way
(Compare and Contrast) 15–16
Possible answers
> **E-mail**: faster, need computer, need Internet, not always private, can break down
> **Mail sent with postage stamps**: can write personal signature, can send photos without special equipment, don't have to worry about others reading and storing information
> **Both**: send messages, give information, can send information across great distances

A Honey of a Job (Reading for Details) 17–18
1. 2 stomachs
2. between 100 and 200
3. 12
4. Utah: The Beehive State
5. A bee should be drawn in South Dakota, Florida, and California.

Answer Key

Native Americans of the Southwest (Reading for Details) 19–20
1. Basket or piece of pottery should appear on the following: Colorado, Arizona, New Mexico, and Mexico.
2. Answers will vary, but student's pottery illustration should match student's story details.

Dancing the Day Away (Picture Clues) 21–22
1. A.
2. The Round dance
3. B.
4. The Waggle dance
5. Drawings will vary.

Landforms (Picture Clues) 23–24
1. mountain
2. plain
3. plateau
4. volcano
5. valley
6. swamp
7. island
8. peninsula
9. strait
10. isthmus

My, How You've Changed! (Sequencing) 25
First—egg
Second—larva
Third—pupa
Fourth—adult

Eruption (Sequencing) 26–27
1. 4, 1, 3, 2
2. True
3. False
4. False
5. True

Warning! Warning! (Sequencing) 28
3 Cooler air moves in.
5 Hurricane warnings are issued.
1 Summer begins.
4 The air begins to spin.
2 A low–pressure area forms above the waves.

Putting It All Together (Sequencing) 29
1. Snap the table legs into the tabletop; this is number 2, and number 2 is the second step.
2. Before; this is number 3, and the step for screwing in the small screws is number 4.
3. Possible answer:
   If all the pieces are not there and she begins, she will spend time on work that she cannot finish. She might put the screws into two cups.
4. Answers will vary, but each paragraph should include a topic sentence and should tell the steps in the correct order. They should include the time–order words from the question.

Two Acts and a Party (Sequencing) 30
3. Stamp Act was repealed.
2. Sons of Liberty formed.
1. Stamp Act was passed.
5. Boston Tea Party occurred.
4. Townshend Acts were passed.

Radio: How Did It Begin? (Sequencing) 31–32
2. Thirty radio stations were broadcasting.
1. Marconi came to the United States.
6. Laws for radio broadcasting were passed.
5. President Roosevelt announces the attack on Pearl Harbor.
3. 550 radio stations were broadcasting.
4. The radio broadcast of the "War of the Worlds" reading.

What Kind of Metamorphosis? (Classifying)........33
Incomplete or Little–by–Little: chinch bug, dragonfly, grasshopper
Complete: housefly, moth, butterfly

Symphony Instruments (Classifying)..............34–35
1. Five instruments
2. Woodwinds
3. Woodwinds
4. Flutes, Woodwinds
5. Clarinets
6. Horns
7. Violas
8. Horns

Answer Key

Music Camp (Classifying) 36
Music Group: clarinet, sheet music, clarinet case
Clothing and Shower Group: shirt, shorts, shampoo
Reading and Writing Group: journal, stationery, magazine

All About Bugs (Table of Contents) 37–38
1. b
2. d
3. a
4. d
5. d
6. b
7. a

Chapter Chooser (Table of Contents) 39–40
1. Chapter 1—because this chapter gives information about types of treasures
2. Chapter 4—because this chapter tells about causes
3. Chapter 3
4. Chapter 4
5. Chapters 1 and 5
6. 91
7. Chapter 5
8. Chapters 7 and 8
9. Chapter 3
10. Glossary

Right Back at You! (Author's Purpose) 41
1. To give you information about bats; reasons will vary, but should show that the author gave facts
2. Answers will vary, but should show a primary purpose of informing, not persuading, entertaining, or expressing feelings.

Mr. Wong's Assignment (Following Directions) ..42
The completed sheet should show no writing except for the student's name above the directions. The response should reflect the importance of following directions.

Map Symbols (Following Directions) 43–44
Map A

Map B

Map C

Stamp Art (Following Directions) 45–46
Stamps will vary, but should depict the following:
1997—Bridge in orange or gold, green hill on left, upper right corner: USA 20, blue background
1998—Skier with black skis, purple background, lower right corner shows USA above 32
1999—Orange and black butterfly, top left corner 33 USA
2000—Purple background, happy snake in orange, green, and blue, green leaves around snake, lower right corner: 34, bottoms of letters USA facing right edge, HAPPY NEW YEAR! in upper right.

Coaching Your Systems (Reading for Information)...........................47–48
1. cerebellum
2. medulla
3. cerebrum
4. cerebellum
5. cerebrum
6. medulla

Answer Key

Food Pyramid (Interpreting Graphs) 49
1. Fruit—1
2. Milk—2, 8, 12
3. Fats and Sweets—3, 11
4. Vegetable—4, 9
5. Meat—5, 10
6. Grain—6, 7

On the Richter Scale (Interpreting Graphs) 50–51
1. There are on the annual average 800 earthquakes at 5.0–5.9. Chart A has the answer.
2. 8,140 earthquakes at 4.0–4.9 on the Richter Scale.
3. It can cause a great deal of damage in a large area.
4. The year 2000 had the most. Chart B has the answer.
5. Most common = 3.1–3.9
   Least common = 8.0–greater
   Chart A has the answer.

Charting Hurricanes (Interpreting Graphs) 52
1. Galveston Storm, Alicia; 1900, 1983
2. by date—because the earliest storm is listed first and the years are listed in order
3. Gilbert, 1988; Hugo, 1989
4. The Galveston Storm—Galveston is a city, not a person's name.
5. The Galveston Storm

How Strong Was That Hurricane?
(Interpreting Graphs) 53
1. category 3 hurricane
2. No
3. tropical
4. category 5
5. tropical depression or TD category

Energy Origins (Interpreting Graphs) 54
1. Canada
2. France/India
3. Japan
4. India and France
5. China or Norway

Dance School (Interpreting Graphs) 55
1. ballet; Chart A because the title is Types of Dance Classes
2. fewer; Chart B because the title is Number of Students from Each Grade Taking Classes

3. jazz and disco
4. ballet and tap; there are more students taking these types of classes than any other.

Yum! It Came from Milk! (Interpreting Graphs) 56
1. Year 6
2. Year 4
3. Years 1 and 2
4. Year 3
5. 1,780 gallons (6,737 liters)
6. Cheddar cheese
7. Swiss
8. Other Italian and Other American
9. 30.6%

Latitude Attitude (Interpreting Graphs) 57
1. Arctic Circle; it's farther from the equator.
2. Yes; they are the same distance from the equator
3. Equator

Time Zones (Interpreting Graphs) 58
1. Montana, Wyoming
2. 8:00 p.m.
3. 7:00 p.m.
4. Eastern standard time
5. Answer should reflect time zone of student's state.

Chomp Down on This! (Critical Thinking) 59
1. A
2. incisors—because they are in front
3. carrot—because it is a vegetable and not a sugary snack.
4. tell an adult—because he should be seen right away
5. B

Promises, Promises (Critical Thinking) 60
PUFFING: You'll never find a better pair of inline skates. People love our jeans.
BETTER BE TRUE: This shirt is made of cotton. There is no fat in our cookies.

Students' own advertisement statements should fit in the category in which each is written.

Answer Key

Return to Sender (Critical Thinking) 61
Letter B. Reasons will vary, but students should include specific examples from both letters.

Ellis Island (Critical Thinking)........................62–63
Answers will vary, but should show an understanding of protecting the United States and making certain that the immigrant could survive in the United States. Sample answers follow.
1. Need to know for records.
2. Need to know country of origin for records.
3. Is the immigrant on his or her own or supported by someone?
4. Is the person healthy?
5. Is the person of good character?
6. Might this person cause problems for the government?
7. Does the person need immediate assistance?
8. Where does the immigrant plan to live?
9. Is the immigrant prepared to get to his or her destination?
10. Does the immigrant have a means of support?

   Journal Entry: Answers will vary, but should include feelings that a frightened, displaced immigrant would likely have.

What Do You Think? (Fact or Opinion) 64
1. Opinion
2. Fact
3. Opinion
4. Opinion
5. Fact
6. Fact
7. Opinion
8. Fact
9. Fact
10. Opinion
11. Opinion
12. Fact
13. Answers will vary.
14. Answers will vary.

How's the Weather? (Fact or Opinion) 65
1. Opinion
2. Fact
3. Fact
4. Opinion
5. Opinion
6. Fact
7. Opinion
8. Fact
9. Opinion
10. Opinion
11. Fact
12. Opinion
13. Fact
14. Fact
15. Fact

Is That a Fact? (Fact or Opinion) 66
1. Fact
2. Opinion
3. Opinion
4. Fact
5. Opinion
6. Fact
7. Fact
8. Opinion
9. Fact
10. Fact
11. Opinion
12. Opinion

It's Simple (Inferencing) 67–70
1. lever
2. inclined plane
3. screw
4. pulley
5. wedge
6. wheel and axle
7. pulley
8. lever
9. wheel and axle
10. inclined plane
11. wedge
12. screw

Fossil-ific! (Inferencing) 71
1. Possible answer: Mold, cast, and trace fossils all tell us more about the creatures and plants of the past.
2. Trace—because it was left behind by the animal
3. Cast—because the fossil is the shape of the plant

Answer Key

Of the People, by the People... (Inferencing) 72

1. Answers will vary, but should contain the idea that as president of the United States, Lincoln was greatly effected by the deaths of many American people.
2. Soldiers fought and many people died there.
3. Answers will vary, but should include terms such as respect, honor, and courage.
4. Answers will vary, but should show critical thinking, rather than literal interpretation.

The Statue of Liberty (Inferencing) 73–74

1. Declaration of Independence; the fight for American independence
2. No, the 100–year birthday was celebrated in 1876.
3. Four months; this time is equal to one-third of a year
4. index finger
5. nose
6. nose
7. 111'1" or 33.86 m

How Does That Work? (Cause and Effect) .. 75–76

1. the tongs opening
2. the man's head falling on something soft
3. Possible answers
   Cause: Man's foot hits lever. **Effect**: Glove goes near turtle's mouth.
   Cause: Glove goes near turtle's mouth. **Effect**: Turtle leans forward.
   Cause: Turtle leans forward to bite glove. **Effect**: Tongs open.
4. Drawings will vary, but should show at least three causes and their effects.

Renewable Resources (Cause and Effect) 77

Possible answers
   Cause: Dam is built. **Effect**: Water falls over dam.
   Cause: Water falls onto turbine blades. **Effect**: Turbine blades spin.
   Cause: Turbine blades spin. **Effect**: Energy goes to generator.

Alexander Graham Bell (Cause and Effect) ..78–79

1. Answers will vary, but should show the impact of improved communication, including ideas such as: improving health care, improving safety, allowing family members who are far away from one another to communicate more easily, improving business.
2. 1847—Bell is born.
   1870—Bell goes to Canada with his parents.
   1874—Bell thinks of the idea for the phone.
   1876—Bell says, "Mr. Watson. Come here; I want you."
   1888—Begins the National Geographic Society
   1922—Bell passes away.

The Great Lakes (Cause and Effect) 80–81

Possible answers
   Cause: Temperatures grew colder. **Effect**: Glaciers formed.
   Cause: Glaciers moved. **Effect**: Rocks and dirt were picked up and shoved forward.
   Cause: Temperatures warmed. **Effect**: Glaciers melted and filled holes to form lakes.

Preparing for an Eruption (Context Clues) 82

1. D
2. Because the passage says that the signs came in the fall.
3. B
4. Because dogs barked and pawed at the ground, snakes slithered onto land, and birds flew away.

Artists and Their Art (Context Clues) 83–84

Answers will vary, but should reflect the style described for each artist.

Preparing for an Earthquake (Main Idea and Details) 85–86

1. People can learn from past earthquakes and prepare for future earthquakes.
2. **Second paragraph**: Everyone in California, and in other areas where earthquakes can happen, should be prepared.
   Third paragraph: The American Red Cross has good advice to help people prepare.
   Fourth paragraph: Have a Home Earthquake Plan.
   Fifth paragraph: Practice DROP, COVER, and HOLD ON!
   Sixth paragraph: Keep your home safe.
   Last paragraph (conclusion): Keep a supply kit in your home and car.

Answer Key

**Here Comes the Sun
(Main Idea and Details)** 87

1. The Mayan civilization might have been destroyed by drought.
2. Answers will vary, but should include any ideas from the paragraph that are not the main idea.
3. Answers will vary, but should reflect the main topic of the paragraph.

A Trip Through the Ages (Timelines) 88–89

1. After
2. Cenozoic
3. Cenozoic
4. No. There was only one continent on Earth at that time.
5. No. Creatures had no backbones during that time.
6. No. Dinosaurs were extinct before the Cenezoic Era.
7. Timelines will vary, but should show basic understanding of chronology of timeline and include at least four important events.

Thomas Jefferson (Timelines) 90

Answers will vary, but might include:
> 1733–born
> 1762–graduated from College of William and Mary
> 1779–became governor of Virginia
> 1783–became member of Continental Congress
> 1785–became minister to France
> 1790–became Secretary of State
> 1797–became vice president
> 1801–became President of the United States
> 1826–passed away

Declaration of Independence (Timelines) 91–92

1. b
2. d
3. c
4. a
5. c

The Beginning of the Internet (Timelines) 93

1. 1994—answer should include why it was important.
2. after

3. President Dwight D. Eisenhower set up government agency for technology.
4. A computer network for communities and schools was planned.
5. President Dwight D. Eisenhower set up a government agency for technology.
   A computer network for communities and schools was planned.

Fine Composers (Timelines) 94

1. Mozart
2. before
3. 27
4. 21
5. Schubert

**Ms. Domingo's Research Hunt
(Using Reference Materials)** 95–96

1. zip code guide
2. dictionary
3. index
4. telephone book
5. table of contents
6. atlas
7. thesaurus
8. atlas

City Beneath the Sea (Reading for Details) 97

1. b
2. c
3. d
4. c

Louisiana Purchase (Reading for Details) 98–99

1. Possible answers: purchased, rather than obtained through war; doubled size of U.S.; gave access to Mississippi River
2. Thomas Jefferson
3. Possible answers: Texas, Louisiana, Oklahoma, New Mexico, Colorado, Wyoming, Montana, North Dakota, South Dakota, Nebraska, Kansas, Arkansas, Missouri, Iowa, Minnesota, Wisconsin
4. Oregon
5. Illinois
6. Mexico

Answer Key

Weekly Assignments (Reading for Details) **100**
1. Yes; he was in class on Monday.
2. On Friday the class will go to the museum.
3. The Talent Show
4. There is a teacher in-service.

Buy It Here! (Reading for Details) **101**
1. No; the coupon was for the first day of the sale only, August 1.
2. No; the shoes must cost at least $20.00.
3. No; the sock special is not available at the Lakeview store, only at the downtown store.
4. No; he must choose socks that cost $2.00 or less.

Recipe for Fun (Reading for Details) **102**
1. They use many low–fat items.
2. Low–fat corn chips, low–fat potato chips, celery
3. Low–fat refried beans
4. No; the recipe doesn't mention baking. It says to chill slightly before eating.

**The Soldier's Lucky Coin
(Author's Purpose)** **103–104**
1. Fact—because the coin was found
2. Yes. The special message that had been on Dixon's coin was on this coin.
3. b
4. Possible answer: The author is not trying to make the reader do anything. The events in the passage really happened, so the passage is not fiction. The passage is not mostly about feelings and can be entertaining.
5. Answers will vary, but the purpose of the first passage should be to give information.

Samuel Morse (Author's Purpose) **105–106**
1. b
2. d
3. d
4. a
5. Answers will vary, but should show originality and detail; answers should explain why the student wants to create the invention and how the invention will help others or solve a problem.

**Native American Biographies
(Organizing Information)** **107–108**
Accomplishment answers will vary. Samples appear below.
Wilma Mankiller   1945   Cherokee   helped health care
Crazy Horse   1849   Lakota   tried to keep Native-American way of life
Chief Joseph   1840   Nez Percé   supported peace
Red Cloud   1822   Lakota   persuaded U.S. to enter into a treaty

U.S. Crops (Interpreting Maps) **109–110**
1. d
2. a
3. c
4. b
5. d
6. a
7. Answers will vary, but should reflect a knowledge that the climate is warmer in the southern U.S. than in the northern U.S.

Regions (Interpreting Maps) **111**
1. South
2. West North Central
3. Sample answer: Florida and Louisiana
4. Sample answer: California
5. Southwest

Escape Routes (Interpreting Maps) **112**
1. a
2. b
3. b
4. a
5. c

**Philo Farnsworth and Television
(Identifying Genre)** **113–114**
1. c
2. b
3. c
4. Drawing should show dollar sign on TV screen
5. Moving images, or pictures, were broken into pinpoints of light. These pinpoints were changed into electrical impulses, or move-ments. Then the impulses were collected by the television set, changed back to light, and people could see the images.

Answer Key

Duke Ellington (Topic Sentences)......................**115**
Answers will vary, but should show a summary of each paragraph. The title should be imaginative and exciting.

Visiting the Big Apple
(Reading for Meaning) **116–117**
1. New York
2. The Big Apple
3. Statue of Liberty, Empire State Building, Ellis Island
4. Central Park
5. Ellis Island; Her relatives came to the United States through Ellis Island.
6. Answers will vary, but should include information from the passage.
7. Appear in a Broadway show
8. In the hotel lobby

Traveling the Internet Highway
(Interpreting Internet Resources) **118–119**
1. Rain Forests
2. Kelp Forests
3. Rain forests; The People for the Rain Forest Association
4. Rain forests; Animals
5. Which Ocean?
6. Rain forests; Internet Search Engines for Students
7. Where to find information on the site
8. Kelp Forests; What Kinds of Plants?
9. Answers will vary, but should include a general title with links to more specific pieces of information relating to the general title.

Name _____

Fossil-ific!

Fossils give information about creatures and plants that lived millions of years ago.

Fossils are most often found in sedimentary rock. Suppose that a plant or animal died millions of years ago near a lake or an ocean. The mud and sand could cover it. Over many years, the mud and sand would harden and form sedimentary rock.

Two kinds of fossils in sedimentary rock are **cast** and **mold**. The mold fossil is a rock with an empty space left after the creature caught in the sediment wore away.

The cast fossil looks like a mold fossil that has been filled. Solid matter from the ground fills the empty space.

Suppose that a dinosaur stepped into soft ground and made a footprint. This would not be a cast or mold fossil. Those come from what is left of plants and creatures when they die. If a dinosaur made a footprint and walked away, the creature would not be there anymore. If the footprint hardened into rock and scientists found it millions of years later, they would be looking at a **trace** fossil.

Directions: Answer the fossil-ific questions below.

1. What is the main idea of this passage?

   _____

2. Suppose that you just found a fossil trail left by wooly mammoths. What kind of fossil is the fossil trail? How do you know?

   _____

   _____

3. Scientists see the shape of a plant against the inside of a cracked rock. What type of fossil is this? How do you know?

   _____

   _____

Name _____

Of the People, by the People...

" . . . the government of the people, by the people, for the people shall not perish from the earth." Who said these famous words? Why? Why are these words such an important part of history?

Many soldiers lost their lives during the Civil War. As a result, a cemetery was created in the city of Gettysburg to honor them. The city of Gettysburg is in Pennsylvania.

During the dedication of the cemetery on November 19, 1863, Abraham Lincoln, the President of the United States, gave a famous speech. Lincoln grieved for the many lost soldiers. His speech told of his sadness. It explained how he respected the soldiers and their courage. The famous words in the first paragraph are from his speech.

Directions: Answer the questions about the passage. You will need to think about what you read in the passage and then think about information you already know.

1. Why was Abraham Lincoln speaking at the cemetery dedication?

   _____

2. Why was the Civil War cemetery in Gettysburg?

   _____

3. Why did Abraham Lincoln want to talk about the soldiers' courage?

   _____

   _____

4. Choose a famous quote and explain what you think it means.

   _____

   _____